Praise for *What Do You Need?*

What Do You Need? is a must-read for anyone who wants to create powerful connections and build community. Lauren Wesley Wilson is a mentor all women will wish they had at work in times of need. In What Do You Need? *Lauren provides us with a window into her dynamic career—from employee at a top communications firm to becoming founder and CEO of ColorComm Corporation. She calls on all women of color to think more strategically about their careers in order to have a fulfilling and rewarding journey.*

— **Huma Abedin**, political strategist and *New York Times* best-selling author of *Both/And*

What Do You Need? gives women of color the power and permission to be conscientiously authentic as they navigate their careers and oftentimes unchartered waters in business. Lauren's commitment to empowering the next generation of leaders with the tools and information to succeed is embedded in every chapter of this book.

— **Star Jones**, attorney, media personality, and TV's *Divorce Court* judge

Lauren Wesley Wilson's What Do You Need? *shares clear pathways for how women of color can harness their personal and professional power. Her writing is thoughtful, honest, and, most of all, you feel how much she wants you to win.*

— **Cleo Wade**, *New York Times* best-selling author of *What the Road Said*

There is nothing more refreshing than learning from someone who has been through it before. What Do You Need? *gives readers the opportunity to be honest with themselves—their successes, their shortcomings, their needs. Lauren provides clear direction for allies to learn how to show up authentically to advocate and support the women of color around them.*

— **Mandy Moore**, Emmy-, Grammy- and Golden Globe–nominated actress

What a novel idea to ask women What Do You Need?
So many of us navigate the journey of our careers facing challenges head-on and trying to figure out what more we need to give, not what we need. In her book, Lauren makes these challenges relatable and offers women of color thoughtful and strategic advice to persevere and succeed.

— **María Elena Salinas**, described as the "Voice of Hispanic America" by *The New York Times* and contributor at *ABC News*

What Do You Need? *It is my favorite question of all time. It represents the "get to the point" of how YOU can achieve your goals! Lauren has given us a primer to the road map, not an exact path but a shared index that translates some of the pitfalls, traps, and high roads on our journey to success!*

— **Michelle Miller**, co-host of *CBS Saturday Morning* and *New York Times* best-selling author of *Belonging*

Success for a woman of color can feel elusive and difficult. What Do You Need? *offers a clear direction on how to find the path to take your career to the next level and not waste time in areas that could be holding you back. Lauren outlines a blueprint for the next generation of leaders.*

— **Deborah Roberts**, co-anchor of *20/20* and *New York Times* best-selling author of *Lessons Learned* and *Cherished*

What Do You Need? *is an honest look into the questions women of color should be asking themselves to achieve a fulfilling career. This book will save readers years of wasted energy and time and will point them in a direction that will lead to achieving their goals.*

— **Michelle Lee**, former editor in chief of *Allure*

What Do You Need?

What Do You Need?

How Women of Color Can
Take Ownership of Their Careers to
Accelerate Their Path to Success

Lauren Wesley Wilson

HAY HOUSE, INC.
Carlsbad, California • New York City
London • Sydney • New Delhi

Project editor: Melody Guy • *Indexer:* Shapiro Indexing Services
Cover design: Kathleen Lynch • *Interior design:* Lisa Vega

Cataloging-in-Publication Data is on file at the Library of Congress

Hardcover ISBN: 978-1-4019-7489-3
E-book ISBN: 978-1-4019-7490-9
Audiobook ISBN: 978-1-4019-7491-6

10 9 8 7 6 5 4 3 2 1

1st edition, April 2024

Printed in the United States of America

SUSTAINABLE
FORESTRY
INITIATIVE

Certified Chain of Custody
Promoting Sustainable Forestry
www.forests.org
SFI-01268

SFI label applies to the text stock

To my parents, who taught me how to use my voice to advocate for what I need.

CONTENTS

INTRODUCTION

It was a Wednesday in May 2011 when I first brought a group of women together in an effort to help advance our collective careers. I was still fairly young—in my twenties, and only a few years out of college—but I knew I didn't want to follow the typical professional development agenda, where attendees sit in the audience, hear from a speaker, wait in line to collect the speaker's business card, and then head back to the office. Those gatherings usually have a jam-packed list of attendees, mostly junior professionals trying to break into an industry or senior leaders supporting a colleague who is speaking, and the only person anyone pays attention to is the speaker, even though the audience members almost always have just as much to offer. The attendees have valuable experience and insight and contacts, and it all goes untapped. Whenever I attended these events (and I did, a lot), I would leave feeling as alone as when I got there, still trying to figure out how to navigate life as a woman of color in the predominantly white communications industry.

I'd gone to countless events that followed that same format, so by the time I was ready to host my own, I had identified the missing piece: community. Other than some post-program time for "mingling" (which was great for people who were already acquainted, but difficult for anyone trying to meet new people, especially one of only a few women of color), most events had no structured opportunity for the audience to get to know each other in a meaningful way or for individuals at different levels of the corporate ladder to exchange advice. And yet the attendees usually had more time and availability to mentor a young professional than any overbooked executive invited to address a crowd, and other times they had even more insight than the speaker herself—maybe they were that person's boss or mentor, with just as much industry knowledge, if not more. Despite this treasure trove of networking gold, people at these events rarely knew who they were sitting next to. They were missing out on opportunities to build their network and gather important information. So my intentions for my first professional luncheon were twofold: bring together women of color, many of whom were the first or only diverse employee in their workplace, and foster true connection among the women in attendance. I wanted everyone to leave feeling like they had a voice at the event and that they took something meaningful away with them. The foundation for these connections was one simple question: *What do you need?*

These four words are surprisingly powerful. For some women of color, they might even feel provocative. Historically, we have not been given permission to think in these terms. We're taught that once we get into an environment where we are in the minority, we should put our head down, do the work, and not ask too many questions or call attention to ourselves. We should focus not on *our* needs, but on the needs of the company and the requirements of our position.

The problem, it turns out, is that just doing good work isn't enough when it comes to succeeding at your profession. Companies don't just want a good worker, they want a cultural "fit," someone who will bring more to the table than just "I did this document and I did it fast." Doing good work is part of the equation, but it will get you only so far. Companies that have hired you already presume that you can do the work because you proved as much during your interview process. That's why you got the job in the first place. The expectations once you're in that desk chair are that you will not only do the job but also embrace the company culture, create relationships across the organization that will help boost productivity, increase the bottom line, and help raise the profile of the company. But here's the catch: your employer isn't going to tell you what you need to do to get ahead—and certainly not *how* to get ahead. Knowing how to do these "extras" means knowing the unwritten rules of getting ahead—rules that are passed down through families or alumni communities or good ol' boy networks, but rarely through managers or HR reps. All of which is to say that if you don't have those connections, you might find yourself learning the hard way—when you're let go, or when it's five years later and you haven't been promoted, or when you get passed over (again!) for the big-budget projects that continually go to your better-connected colleagues.

That's exactly what happened to me. A year into my first job out of grad school, I thought I was doing everything right. I got to the office on time if not early and stayed until six. I said yes to every project that was floated my way and always met my deadlines. I'd been taught that the way to succeed in business was to put my nose to the grindstone and do good work, so you can imagine my surprise during my annual review when I was told that the feedback from others around the office was: "We don't really know Lauren."

What do they mean, they don't know me? I remember thinking. *I arrive every day with a smile. I say good morning. I make the coffee when it's my turn.* I thought I was supposed to come to the office, do my job well, and then go home, because no one ever told me differently. None of my higher-ups had taken me under their wing and let me know I needed to sign up for the company 5K run or volunteer for the holiday party–planning committee in order to get to know other employees. I wasn't clued in to the soft skills needed to get ahead, and now I had been branded, apparently, as "unknowable."

It's often said that women of color have to work twice as hard in their careers to get half as much. And this is true. But it's not necessarily that we have to work twice as hard on our actual work. (Though, to be honest, if you're one of the few people of color in a workspace where layoffs are on the horizon, chances are you're going to be on the chopping block before others unless you are killing it, so make sure everyone knows you are killing it.) We have to work twice as hard to connect with the people around us, because the reality of the workplace, for better or worse, is that people invest their energy in employees who remind them of themselves. And in a world where everyone feels short on time, we often rely on surface-level attributes for those reminders. It's easy to spot someone who is a replica of you—someone who looks the same, or has the same style, or even comes from the same neighborhood or went to the same school. If you're a woman of color working in an environment where the majority of the employees look different from you, it can seem like you're starting two steps behind. Your employer is less likely to seek you out to share advice on how to get ahead at your company. You have to find a way to connect with people with whom you don't have any obvious commonalities. You have to dig deeper, and that takes real effort.

At my first job, one popular after-hours team-building activity was going to professional ice hockey games. I didn't raise my hand to go because I didn't care about ice hockey. I had colleagues who truly liked it, but they also wanted visibility and access. Later I would watch these same employees—mostly white—pounce on opportunities I never got. Not because they were better at their jobs than I was, and not, I don't think, because they were white. It was never as overt as that. It was because, at some point, someone had nurtured them and taught them the unspoken rules of the game, and they had taken the time to play that game. They had gotten to know decision-makers outside of the moments when the decisions were happening, and it was paying off. Needless to say, I didn't last at that job for long.

As my career advanced, I got savvier at navigating the corporate world as a woman of color. And though I got better at the relationship-building piece—volunteering for party-planning committees and kickball leagues—I still didn't have a true mentor. I didn't have someone to guide me or give me the inside scoop on what I needed to do to get ahead. In 2010, I was working at a global communications public relations firm, and my goal was to be in a VP position by age 30. The only problem: there was not a single woman of color at the VP level or above. It's a popular cliché to say that you can't be what you can't see, but it's how I felt back then. How was I going to advance if there had never been a woman of color in any of those roles?

After nearly a year of trying to schedule a face-to-face lunch with a former grad school professor who I thought could be a mentor, I realized there had to be an easier way. I needed guidance from people who had been where I was—people who could give advice on how to bring in business, how to connect better with my manager and clients, how to ask for time off, and how to handle being the only woman of color on the team. By then I'd learned that management wasn't going to teach me how to get ahead. Neither was HR. They were going to wait for me to make mistakes before they coached me on what I needed to do better. The problem, though, is that when you're the only woman of color in a company and you're shouldering the burden of "representing" an entire race of people, you feel like you can't afford to make mistakes. There are too many eyes on you, too many people generalizing your performance to an entire demographic.

And so in 2011, I co-hosted that networking luncheon that was intended to do things differently. It was intended to be an avenue for women of color in communications to come together, get to know each other, and share the information I wish someone had given me back in my first job. Because women of color are often at a disadvantage when it comes to having that outside help. We are more likely to be first generation and less likely to have parents who worked in corporate environments, meaning we're less likely to have the connections or inside advice that are so beneficial when starting careers or trying to advance. We're often the "first" or "only" in our positions—the first woman of color to hold a position, the only one sitting around the conference table. The luncheon I co-hosted was about creating a community in a professional world that could feel especially lonely, and it was about getting everyone the information they needed that they couldn't seem to get elsewhere. Because by that point, I knew what I needed—guidance on the next steps to reach my VP-by-30 goal—but other attendees had different needs, because they were at different places in their careers.

The one thing I knew to be true that afternoon was that everyone in attendance, no matter their position in their organization's hierarchy, had something to give and something to receive. So we went around the room, shared our names and titles, and said what we needed. Out loud. The answers were personal and professional, everything from "I need a contact at *The New York Times*" to "I just moved to D.C. and I need a hairdresser." It was a transformative and fulfilling event for everyone in the room, because they found a community of people who looked like them, and they also got the specific information they were after. Everyone in the room had a voice, added value, and was encouraged to be proactive in a world where they were usually taught to wait their turn, even if, by the time their turn came around, it was too late.

That event was the first of what would become a luncheon series, and eventually an entire platform: ColorComm. The ColorComm luncheons took place quarterly in that first year, and they blended age groups and org charts. Senior leaders gave junior-level employees the wisdom of their experience, and the junior people could say, "Oh, you don't know how to make a media list? Or navigate LinkedIn? This is easy for me; let me help." By 2012, enough people wanted to formalize the program that we went from a luncheon series to a membership program, launching in Washington, D.C., with 40 members and a board of advisors. Over the next few years, we expanded into Chicago, Atlanta, New York, Los Angeles, San Francisco, Dallas, Houston, and Miami. During this growth period, I left my firm to work as a communications director on Capitol Hill and then as a media strategist for President Barack Obama's reelection campaign. After the campaign, I oversaw media strategy and crisis communications at another global firm (think *Scandal*) until 2015, when, one month before my 30th birthday, I left that job to run ColorComm full-time. Today, ColorComm is the nation's leading women's platform addressing diversity and inclusion across the communications, marketing, advertising, and media industries. We have hosted events with speakers including Whoopi Goldberg, Gayle King, Ann Curry, April Ryan, Gloria Steinem, Lisa Ling, and many, many more, connecting people across industries and org charts, and always the driving question is the same: "What do you need?"

ColorComm Corporation's structure unites our professional membership organization, jobs platform, and client service, and serves more than 100,000 professionals across its platforms. When I ask our community why they participate, the most common answer I hear is that they don't know where else to turn. Because the way you get information is by talking to people, and if you aren't already entrenched in a network full of individuals who've already done what you're doing, finding the people with insight and intel to share can be hard. That's where this book comes in. During the nearly 15 years I've spent with ColorComm, I've learned so much from our speakers and members, but I've also experienced it. I've been the first-and-only trying to navigate a complicated work environment, and I've been a CEO, assessing employees at all levels of performance. I've learned the hard way and then found my footing, and I've done the hiring and the inevitable firing. I have spent years talking with insiders, specifically women of color who have navigated these very complicated waters, and I'm here to share the unwritten (until now!) intel that your white colleague might have gotten from his uncle or neighbor or Ivy League mentor. Because that's the leg up we need sometimes—just a peek at what's happening behind the scenes. The info that the employee handbook won't tell you. Want to know how to become the rock star at work, rather than the "good enough" employee? You'll find that here. Wondering why you aren't making more money, or why you've been passed over for a promotion? You'll learn that, too. Curious about those unspoken "soft skills" that no one taught you in school? I got you.

This book is about thinking about your work in a new way. I want you to understand the professional game that's being played all around you, I want you to crack the code of success, and I want you to enjoy yourself along the way. I want you to determine which issues are worth speaking out on and when timing matters. I want you to understand that all battles aren't worth fighting and to be strategic about which battles you choose to occupy your time with.

Women of color account for only 4 percent of C-Suite positions, and that number, of course, needs to change. Yet every day I interact with women of color who are running on the hamster wheel, putting in their time, and not seeing the results in their paycheck or their promotion schedule. More often than not, it's because they don't know the unspoken rules of how to advance and get ahead of red flags in their performance. They don't look at their careers through a business lens because no one ever taught them to. Sometimes it takes so much effort for a woman of color just to get in the door that we forget we need a new set of tools in order to stay inside the four walls. This book will supply strategies I've learned throughout my own career and others shared by ColorComm members and speakers for getting ahead as a woman of color in the workplace. It will help you identify what you need, and teach you how to ask for it.

I should point out that "What do you *need*?" is not the same question as "What do you *want*?" Knowing what you want can be helpful as you think through where you want to work or what career you want to pursue, but once you've signed on for a job, what you want isn't the most important thing. Work environments aren't designed to be customized experiences, which is why there are employee handbooks, clear policies, and procedures in place. But while you can't always get what you want, you should be able to get what you *need* in order to be successful in the position you've been hired for. You should be able to ask for what you need in order to take the next step. So when I urge you to focus on the question of "What do you need?" I'm not saying you should create a laundry list of workplace demands. I'm saying you need to figure out how you can be the most successful in your workplace and in your life, and you can't be afraid to ask for help.

While everyone's individual needs will be different, there are some needs that come up time and again in conversations with ColorComm members. *I need to build a network. I need to ask for a raise. I need my boss to stop assigning me to all the DEI projects. I need to move on.* This book will address all that and more. It will offer all the information that I wish I had when I started out, and the info I wish all ColorComm members had. It will cover topics like imposter syndrome, making a name for yourself, building your network, establishing your value, taking calculated risks, and getting promoted. It will also give practical tips for recognizing when things just aren't working: What are the red flags that indicate a workplace isn't set up for your success? How can you tell if you're wasting your time at a job that won't promote you, or that a company isn't worth your energy? And, for the white allies who want to help create spaces where everyone feels welcome, there will be a section focused on what support looks like, and why it benefits you and your organization.

There's no question that the past few years have brought an increased understanding of the challenges facing women of color in the workplace, as well as a greater focus on supporting and understanding the diversity, equity, and inclusion landscape. If you are reading this book, you already know these challenges. Maybe you face them on a daily basis, or maybe you're trying to be a white ally and want to understand how to better support your colleagues of color. At this point, I'm more interested in focusing on the *how*: how to get ahead, how to claim space, how to succeed in spite of the challenges. I want to empower you to take control of your career in ways you may not have thought of because no one ever took you aside to give you these tips. I want you to figure out what you need to be a success, and, more important, I want you to go out and get it.

PART ONE

Finding Your Place

— 1 —

YOU NEED . . .
TO KNOW IF YOU BELONG

In 2008, just out of graduate school, I got my first full-time job offer. I'd just finished my master's degree in communications at Georgetown University, during which I'd completed internships at two top global PR firms. I knew I was a desirable candidate, but the country was in the middle of a recession and hardly anyone was hiring. When an offer came through for a junior-level position at a mid-sized D.C. communications firm, I slapped on a smile and said, "Where do I sign?" I was living with my aunt in Maryland at the time, contributing what little I could to the rent, so I was just happy to have a paycheck. I didn't think I had the luxury of being choosy.

A year later, I was laid off. That was the job where they said they didn't know me. Yes, I did good work; sure, I always showed up on time and never missed a deadline. But that wasn't enough. I hadn't infiltrated the workplace culture or become a part of the office community. I didn't network or play office politics. I showed up at 9 A.M., did my work and went home at 6 P.M. It was enough to get the job done, but not enough to launch a career. As my boss told me in his office the day I was let go, it wasn't working out.

As I look back on that job now, it's clear that I made my first mistake before I ever stepped foot in the office. I was so desperate for a job that I didn't bother to learn more about the company that I planned to launch my career with. I never stopped to ask: *Do I belong here?*

Obstacles Ahead

I've been grappling with the question of belonging for as long as I can remember. As a Black girl growing up in an upscale suburb of St. Louis, I rarely interacted with other people of color. I went to a small, predominantly white private school, and I got used to being the only Black girl in class, or at the sporting event, or at the party. I was so conditioned to hearing comments like "You're articulate for a Black girl" or "You're pretty for a Black girl" that I almost forgot how offensive they are. When I started considering Spelman College, a women's HBCU, my friends couldn't believe it. "Are you going to fit in?" they asked, because they were used to seeing me amid white faces. "Are you going to belong there?"

"Well, it's a college for Black women," I'd respond. "And I'm a Black woman, so I think I'll fit in."

However, it wasn't quite that easy. After spending 18 years surrounded by white friends, Spelman was an adjustment. Students came from all over the country—there were Black women from Colorado and Rhode Island, with every type of background and interest. I hadn't known that level of diversity existed within the Black community. I hadn't known there were all these Black people who skied, swam, or played field hockey. It was eye-opening, and intimidating, too. I was so used to being the *only*, and in some ways, when that happens, you start to think you're special. You're an asterisk. You forget that there are more of you, and while that was a huge comfort, it took some getting used to. For a while, "Do I belong?" was a question for me at Spelman, too.

But when that first job offer came in, I didn't ask about belonging. If they were willing to pay me, they must have thought I belonged. Or so I figured.

Had I done my homework, I might have known differently. There was nothing inherently wrong with this firm—it wasn't corrupt or overtly racist. There were no unethical workplace practices. But had I taken the time to do a little research, I would have learned that I was only their second Black employee, and that there were no people of color in leadership. I would have understood their conservative values—which were not at all aligned with my own—and taken note of their roster of conservative clients. The company was successful, sure, but it was not set up for my success.

"Do I belong here?" is a question many women of color ask themselves on an almost-daily basis. In workplaces, in classrooms, in social spaces. We are constantly taking the temperature in the room, figuring out if we fit in and if we'll be welcomed. The answer, in an ideal world, should always be yes. You belong in whatever environment you choose to inhabit, and you should take up space, bring your full self to work, and know your worth. In reality, though, the answer is sometimes no. Some spaces are not set up for you to thrive. Some are not the right fit, or they require so much of your time and energy—without giving you anything in return—that they're an unnecessary lift. As much as you deserve to feel supported wherever you choose to work, trying to change an entire environment on your own is a Herculean task. And it might not be worth shouldering that burden on your own.

Even in the best workplaces, women of color face disproportionate challenges. Every year the management consulting firm McKinsey & Company teams up with the nonprofit LeanIn.Org to produce what's called the *Women in the Workplace* report, with much of the research focused on the experience of women of color specifically. The results, quite frankly, are often disheartening, though they won't come as a surprise to any of us who have been in the trenches. According to the 2022 report, women of color are less likely to be promoted than our male or white female counterparts. (The hype here is often focused on the C-Suite, where only 1 in 20 executives are women of color. But the disparity starts early: for every 100 men promoted out of entry-level positions, only 87 women, and 82 women of color, get the same bump.) We are less likely to have senior colleagues advocate for us and less likely to be promoted. Black women make 67 cents to every white man's dollar, and for Hispanic women that gap is even bigger—only 54 cents on the white man's dollar. (There is a pay gap for white women, too, but it's significantly less: 73 cents for every dollar earned by white men.) We are judged more harshly for our mistakes. We are far more likely to be on the receiving end of microaggressions, those behaviors that seem entirely intended to make us feel othered or different. According to the 2022 report, Latinas and Black women are less likely to report that their manager supports their career development; Asian and Black women are less likely to have strong allies on their team; Latinas and Asian women are more likely to hear someone comment on their nationality (questions like "Where are you really from?" are still uttered in office places). Being interrupted, having our qualifications questioned, being told we "should smile more" or that we "speak really well"— all of this is piled on in addition to our regular workload, and it makes women of color more likely to experience burnout or job discontent. And yet! According to the same research, despite all these challenges, women of color are more eager to get ahead. A full 41 percent of women of color want to be top executives, compared with 27 percent of white women.

Despite that desire, we are wholly underrepresented. In any given office space, women of color are often the first or the only, sometimes in two different dimensions. It's called the Double Minority Tax: we're the only woman and the only person of color, which means we are assigned the added work of representing, on our own, two entirely different groups. In fact, one in eight women of color still find herself to be both the only woman *and* the only person of her race in any given meeting or office place. In her memoir, *Year of Yes*, Shonda Rhimes coined the term "F.O.D.—a First. Only. Different."

When you are the first or only, everything is harder. It just is. It takes more work to get in the door, and once you do, people look at you and wonder, *How did you get here? Did you earn it, or are you a diversity hire?* Finding a mentor takes more effort. Your mistakes draw more eyeballs. Your lived experiences are different, which means you approach challenges differently and may have to work harder to convince people of your solutions. There might be racism in the workplace, either overt or more quiet. Microaggressions are rampant and go largely unnoticed by those not on the receiving end, but they hinder your productivity and ultimately the company's. Questions about where you're from, your hairstyle, or your name may be hidden under the guise of curiosity, but that curiosity sends a clear message: you are different from us.

What Does It Mean to Belong?

All of these challenges bring up more questions of belonging: Where are the others? Will it always be this way? How do I create space for change so that there can be more than the one token woman of color in this space? Sometimes these questions are worth investigating, but a company should earn the extra work it will require of you.

Questions of belonging come up not only because women of color want to fit in. It's not merely an issue of looking like the person next to you, although it's certainly nice to not always be the only one or to have role models who came before you who prove success is possible. The true reason we ask if we belong is that we want to thrive. We want to succeed and reach our potential and contribute in ways we know we are capable of. And sometimes that's possible even *if* we are the first or only.

When women of color ask "Do I belong here?" what we are really asking is, "Will I be accepted? If I am doing good work, will I be given the same opportunities to advance as the people around me? Will I be included in decision-making discussions when appropriate?" This is not a question of race, it's a question of respect. We want to be included and considered when the organization plans team-building events or celebrations, and not only when those events are gender or race related. We want to know we aren't seen only as the Black employee or Asian employee or Latina employee or female employee, but that we're recognized for our personal interests and professional accomplishments, too. In fact, a 2018 study of over 7,000 workers found that a sense of belonging was the metric most strongly and consistently tied to employee experience and engagement.[1] In this study, conducted by employee experience platform Culture Amp and DEI consultancy

Paradigm, *belonging* was defined as "the feeling of security and support one gets when there is a sense of acceptance, inclusion, and identity for a member of a certain group or place." To belong is to be seen, heard, respected, and valued. These are pretty simple concepts, but they aren't a given in every office space. Far from it.

It would have been hard for me to answer questions about workplace advancement and inclusion before I accepted that first public affairs job. You can never know everything about a company before you take your space within its four walls (or, increasingly, its virtual walls). But I could have read up on the strategic plan, or gotten a better sense of the org chart. Part of understanding whether you will be successful is understanding what the company has done before your arrival—has there ever been a person of color in leadership? Do they have a team focused on diversity, equity, and inclusion? If they do, has it been there awhile, or was it a slapdash team thrown together in response to current events? Does that team have a budget? Do they move the needle or are they merely in check-the-box roles?

There will be instances when the answers to all these questions are no—*no*, they haven't had diverse leaders; *no*, they don't seem to care about changing that—but it's your dream job, and so you decide to move forward anyway. There are some environments worth fighting for. You will be the trailblazer, the one who creates change, because this is *the* place where you want to work. That's your decision, and it might pay off. I hope it does. Even in those cases, you're starting off on a better foot when you come equipped with information. Knowledge is power. When you know what you're getting into, you adjust accordingly.

The truth is, for me, that first company wasn't my dream job. It was a job. And that's the case more often than not.

In those instances, the answers to your questions become even more telling. If a company already has women of color in leadership, on important accounts, or getting promoted, then at least that's a landscape that's already been navigated. If not, you might want to think twice, because you may not want to solve all these problems for them.

The Setup for Success

Just as important as understanding a company's history is understanding its current state of affairs. When I look back at that first job, the "woulda, coulda, shoulda" that plagues me is this: I should have spoken to another employee (outside of the interviewers) before I accepted the job. It didn't have to be an employee of color—considering that there were barely a handful of us, that would have been tough—but I should have connected with someone to at least ask one simple question: What is it like to work there?

Belonging at a company isn't just about looking the part. In fact, it's about so much more than that. Belonging involves integrating yourself into the company culture, knowing the right people, understanding the politics. It's about understanding what makes a person successful at that specific organization so you have a clear path. And no one is going to give you that information during your interview process. HR will sit you down and let you know when you've messed up, but they won't school you on the soft skills needed to get ahead. When you talk to HR, or interview with a potential manager, they might say "Success at this company is about being a team player!" Or "All it takes to succeed here is to do good work." But the truth is, we can all perform. I think about the jobs I've held, many of which were at global companies. To get inside those walls is hard; it takes a rigorous interview process and hours of meetings and interfacing with individuals up and down the corporate ladder. By the time I was sitting at my desk, I knew I was smart and capable, because otherwise I wouldn't have been there. And that's true in any job—you got the offer, so clearly you have proven that you can handle the work. Most of the time, that won't be the thing that keeps you from succeeding. What will keep you from succeeding is not knowing the playbook. I'm not talking about the company handbook that HR hands you when you sign your offer letter. I'm talking about the unwritten playbook. And let me assure you, every organization has one, and each is a little bit different. What will get you ahead at one company can mean your demise at another, so this is the knowledge you need.

I liken it to candy. Sure, it's a type of treat, an umbrella category, but not all candy is the same. There's chocolate candy, gummy candy, hard candy, caramels. Corporate America, any workplace really, is the same. The framework is similar at each place, there are general rules that apply no matter where you work, and yet every company that hires you will have its own flavor. There will be tricks to getting ahead in that space. Maybe at your particular company only the big clients matter. Maybe you need to know somebody, because nepotism, or having the right connections, is the only way to make an impression. It could be that they're all about an Ivy League education—if you don't have that, good luck, because they treat everyone else like second-class citizens. It could be that one particular senior leader has a lot of pull, so getting on her good side is your ticket to the top; or maybe they say you start at 9, but they really want to see you at 8:30, or after-work happy hours are supposedly optional, but the higher-ups are silently taking stock of who's there.

Some of these factors are outside your control—you either went to an Ivy League school or you didn't; you either have a neighbor who works in the C-Suite or you don't—but some of them you can figure out. If you know which clients to focus on or which after-work get-together to attend, you can carve out a space for yourself. You can act like you belong until eventually you really do.

It would be nice, perhaps, if none of this mattered, if success was about work product and all else was an even playing field. But if you're reading this book, you already know that's not the case, and never has been.

If you're thinking at this point, *Oh that's not my company. Where I work it's all about output*, I have news for you. People are "playing the game," whether you know it or not. They are going to happy hours or convening the meeting before the meeting, and you aren't a part of it. Just because you don't see it doesn't mean it isn't happening, so let's get you on the inside!

When I took that first job, I was passionate about PR and the communications industry. I had no trouble doing the work—I was tasked with writing press releases and making media lists and planning trade shows. I knew how to work in Excel. I was a good writer. My challenge was never the work. I struggled at that job because of the things I did not know, in part because I never asked. If I had sought out a current employee to give me the rules of the road, I might have known that Client X was considered the most important, so I shouldn't be devoting so much work time to Client Y. Instead, I got piercing looks that said *Hmmm, she doesn't know what she's doing*. I might have known that when folks gathered around the watercooler, they weren't just talking about what happened on last night's episode of *Real Housewives*. They were having "the meeting behind the meeting," where everyone would get on board with whatever plan was being pitched in the conference room that afternoon (more on this later, but trust me, it's happening). But I didn't know, so instead I'd attend the meeting, give my own opinion—which of course contradicted what everyone else had already agreed to—and single myself out, again, in an environment where I was already on an island. If I'd asked some more questions beforehand, I might have known that the connections between senior leaders and junior-level employees were happening in the stands of those Washington Capitals games, and that I should raise my hand to go whether I cared about hockey or not. I was looking at those outings thinking, *How nice, they must all like hockey. They must all be good friends.* I didn't realize that this was where the team was connecting on a human level, that people were finding their mentors and exchanging information right there at the Capital One Arena. I didn't know any better, because no one ever told me any better.

In a predominantly white company, gathering this information is always hardest for women of color. People want to help out the new employee who reminds them of a younger version of themselves. They seek out that person, take them under their wing, share with them their secrets of success. If nobody sees themselves in us, it's likely no one is popping by our desk and inviting us to coffee or offering us a sneak peek behind the scenes. I'll get more into the importance of finding these mentors and sponsors in a later chapter, but for now, when you're still just trying to figure out if you belong, I want you to be proactive. When you are offered the job, get on LinkedIn. Do you have a friend of a friend of a friend who works there? If so, ask for an intro. If you can't find a connection, ask your hiring manager if there's an employee at your level that you can speak with. Some of the information about your company should be readily available. You should be able to figure out if there are other women of color in the workplace or on the leadership team. A company's DEI initiatives should be easy enough to find on their website or with a Google search. But some of the other stuff, the "what it takes to get ahead here" information that only the insiders know, that may be harder to come by. If you can't get it before you accept the job—or if you, like I once did, feel like you can't turn down a paycheck—make it a point to arrive on your first day with your eyes and ears open. It's too easy to go in with a blind eye, excited to have a job but with no plan to figure out how the company works or who you need to get to know. Learning about what makes a company tick, how it operates, and who gets ahead is just as important as understanding the work. You need to arrive every day with that at the forefront of your mind.

All that said, as you do your due diligence, it's important to note: no company is perfect. A lot of these organizations have been around for decades and yet they are just now starting to play catch-up on the work that ColorComm started nearly 15 years ago. You may find that they excel in some areas—maybe they have improved hiring practices and implemented DEI training—but are still falling short in others, like the diversity of their C-Suite. Only you know what's enough for you, and we should all be clear on our nonnegotiables, but if you get the sense that an organization is making progress and you can feel their investment in your success, recognize that they are trying.

It's all too common in these post-pandemic times for employees—especially junior ones—to write off a company because it doesn't meet all the criteria on their "where to work" checklist. But we have to have a level of acceptance for a company's shortcomings. No workplace will be without challenges. Offices are not tailored to each specific employee, and companies can't cater to each person's individual needs when there are hundreds of workers on their payroll. Still, a company, or the people at a company, should be able to show an investment in your success and an eagerness to include you. If you are invited to be on the holiday party-planning committee, where everyone else is white, it might show that they realize they want and need a diverse perspective. At least someone in that room is making an effort. If you are being invited into those watercooler conversations, or you're being paired with a mentor—whether it's a work superior or a peer who's been at the company awhile—then the company is putting intention into helping you succeed. I'm not saying any one of those actions is enough, or that a person who extends an invitation has suddenly saved the day, but they're trying. You will never be entirely free from the occasional mishap or faux pas that happens whenever two or more people share the same space, especially when those two people come from different backgrounds, but you can feel the difference between an honest mistake and a lack of investment. When you can at least see that the people at this company want you there, and they want you to do well . . . well, it's a start.

Bring Your Full Self to Work?

Let's say you've done your research, and you've decided that yes, this is a company that wants me—and they want me for the right reasons. They want my intelligence and experience, they want my diverse perspective, and they think I can improve their bottom line and make an impact. I belong at this job, and I'm going to take it.

Great! Now it's time to show up. There's been a lot of talk over the last few years about "bringing your full self to work." The idea is that you arrive as your most authentic self—you don't assimilate into the culture. Who you are at home is who you are at the office. You don't put up a shield, you showcase your vulnerabilities, you are honest about your perspectives and opinions and you share them without reserve. The idea is that bringing your full self will create safer and more productive workplaces. It's a nice sentiment, if a little idealistic.

Here's the thing about bringing your full self to work: it's a fine line for any employee, and an extra fine one for a woman of color. First, ask yourself. What does your full self look like? Not every environment is structured for every part of yourself. You don't need to be bringing your dating woes to the office. No one needs to get in on your family drama. I was taught at an early age not to over-share, to keep my family and financial business to myself when in a place of business. But people *do* want to know who you are. They want to get to know you on a personal level, to connect with you and relate to you, so if you seem like you're not bringing *any* of yourself to work—if you appear to be going through the motions, clocking in and clocking out without stopping to chat or making an effort to show who you are—someone will say they don't know you. Still, if you start to advertise your problems, or go off too much about your personal life, you could quickly be labeled unprofessional. Like I said, a fine line.

Listen, the person who wrote the book on bringing your whole self to work, which is literally called *Bring Your Whole Self to Work*, is a white man. I'm sure his intentions were good. But his experience is not our experience. In a 2020 study commissioned by *Essence*, 80 percent of Black women surveyed said they felt it necessary to adjust their personalities to succeed at work. Fifty-seven percent said they felt a need to change their physical appearance to be promoted, whether that meant straightening their hair or adhering to a certain style of dress. Women of color across the board feel far less free to bring their whole selves to work because for decades we've been told not to. I like to think we're making strides on all these factors, but the truth is that workplaces have norms, and it does help to adhere to them.

And frankly, I don't think anyone needs to come to the office completely embracing their most authentic self. It's still a place of business. Your company is paying you to be there, and they expect their employees to present and behave in a certain way. If you're someone who is chronically late, you can't just roll in at 10 for a 9 A.M. start time and say, "This is my whole self!" If you're most comfortable in pajamas, that doesn't really matter. You can't wear them and still expect to be taken seriously. People like to test work boundaries more and more these days, but we need to be practical and realistic. Bringing your full self to work has consequences—people make snap judgments about everyone all the time—so there is an upside to keeping things professional. I liken it to being an athlete. When you are suiting up for a game, you don't bring all your baggage onto the field. You focus on the game at hand, and while the game clock is running, everything else is secondary.

So how about this: bring some of yourself to work. Your professional self. Enough of yourself that people can connect with you over a shared love of reading or cooking or cycling. Enough to empower your colleagues to say that they "know you" and back that up with an anecdote or two. And once you've climbed the ranks, after you've paid your dues and shown that you can bring in big money and improve the bottom line? You'll have earned the right to bring your *whole* self, or at least a bit more of yourself, just as you'll have earned the right to a higher salary. That same *Essence* survey found that 39 percent of Black women in the C-Suite openly share the traits that differentiate themselves from others. What companies want most of all, remember, is someone who can increase revenue. That, more than anything, will tell them you belong.

Battling Impostor Syndrome

Now, let's consider a different scenario. You've looked into a company and decided that no, *I don't belong. This isn't the place for me. I can't succeed here.* Before you pass on a job or write off a company, I want you to be sure those cues are coming from the outside rather than the inside. It's one thing to doubt an organization—especially one that has given no indication of its investment in your success—but it's another thing entirely to doubt yourself. It's common for women, especially high-achieving women, to question their abilities. We wonder if we are deserving of whatever accolades we've received. Studies show that this kind of self-doubt, otherwise known as impostor syndrome, plagues women of color more than white women—and how could it not? If you're one of the first or the only woman who looks like you in a given room, it's easy to wonder if you somehow pulled a fast one. Pile on overt or covert racism and gender inequality and pay inequity and microaggressions, and even the most confident among us can start to question our own self-worth or shy away from asking for the support we need to advance in a given space. Call attention to ourselves, and we might be found out! But if the message that you can't succeed is coming from your own self-doubt, I want you to seek out support or a cheerleader—a friend, family member, a network like ColorComm. Don't let it keep you from pursuing a job you want and you've earned. Easier said than done, I know, but facing impostor syndrome head-on will allow you to stay in a space long enough to realize that you're there because you've earned it.

Here's the truth: one way or another, you will find out if you belong in any given work environment. My hope is that with this book, you can figure it out sooner rather than later, and on your own terms, because way too often people of color learn when it's already too late. We don't ask questions ahead of time for fear of appearing needy or nosy or demanding. We worry that we'll be perceived as ungrateful, or that speaking up will hinder our advancement. Fast-forward a couple of years, and we're suddenly being let go, or we've dedicated years to a place that isn't promoting us or investing in us. And then, when we ask for candid feedback on what we did wrong or how we can improve, we are told that we "just aren't a fit." I cannot tell you how often the women of color in my life have heard that line. In today's environment especially, managers are more nervous than ever about coming off as racist or having their words taken the wrong way, so instead of giving clear direction, they say nothing of substance and throw jargon at the problem. In fact, the way in which feedback is delivered can be another good clue as to whether or not you belong in a given workspace. To be clear, belonging in a work environment doesn't mean getting only positive feedback. Most people in any office have things they do well and things they can improve on. If you're asking for feedback and you're getting a whole lot of "Everything is fine" in response, it might be time to go on high alert. More often than not, "everything is fine" doesn't mean *everything is fine*; "everything is fine" means *I don't want to have this conversation.*

When I was at that first job, I checked in with my boss every couple of months on my way to the annual performance review. I wanted to know how I was doing, what I could do better, and how I could get ahead. Yet every time we met, I was told, "Everything is great." Then, when review time finally came along, the story was very different from "You're doing fine." It was "This isn't working out." It felt like a classic bait and switch.

What I've learned, and what I've heard from so many women at ColorComm, is that it's very hard for us to get candid feedback on our work because people want to avoid conflict with people of color. We get fake or sugar-coated commentary, which is not helpful if you're trying to progress. If someone is truly invested in you, you will get clear and specific notes on what you are doing well and what you can do better, and you'll get it on a reasonable schedule. You will be given a window of time that allows you to improve if necessary so that you can meet your promotion time line or salary bump goals. If someone waits to tell you everything you need to do to improve until the day before your review? That person is looking to create a paper trail. They don't want to help you succeed; they want to cover their own ass so they can't be accused of bias when bad news is delivered.

The good news, of course, is that fit goes both ways. You don't have to wait until your boss or manager tells you it's not working. You can decide that on your own, and I hope you do. Because you can use all the tips I'm going to lay out in the chapters to come, but if you're working in an environment where you don't belong—for reasons of race or gender or socioeconomic status, or because you can't navigate the company's particular road map for success—you'll be spinning your wheels regardless. And as much as we know the systems need to change, they are not going to do so overnight. That will happen incrementally. Going in every day and thinking that you alone are going to make profound advancements on diversity issues is not realistic. There's no faster way to burn out, and then you're just another person of color who left after two years.

I know it's popular to say "You belong everywhere!" and yes, that would be nice. But honestly, it's like dating. There will always be people who aren't right for you, and most of the time, it's not you, it's them. Trying to force yourself into a workspace that will never be amenable to you will only make your work life more difficult at a time when it doesn't have to be. Work shouldn't be easy, but it shouldn't feel like you're always swimming upstream. Constantly fighting to make an environment accept you or twiddling your thumbs waiting for it to become more fair—neither of those approaches is going to serve you in the long run. So pay attention from the outset, because this is a book about the unspoken rules of the career long game. If you don't belong in the space where you work, the game was rigged before you even started playing.

— 2 —

YOU NEED . . .
TO MAKE A NAME
FOR YOURSELF

When I started ColorComm, I was only a few years into my professional career. I was working at a global PR firm, and if I knew one thing by then it was that if I wanted to be successful, I needed to build relationships. I needed to know people, and much more important, I needed people to know me. Nearly 15 years after our first luncheon, ColorComm has changed and grown, but our core mission is still the same today as it was back then: to create mentorships, business relationships, and friendships. To create a community of women who can work together through collaboration and who will speak each other's names aloud when that person isn't in the room. If there's one thing all success relies on, relationships are it.

I've already mentioned the importance of being *known* where you work. If your colleagues or superiors feel like they don't know you, they're less likely to vouch for you. And the less likely they are to vouch for you, the more dispensable you seem to the company. When I say "know you," I mean that people feel like you're their "friend," or at least that they're friendly enough with you that they have something positive to say when your name comes up. (I'm putting *"friend"* in quotes here because a work friend is different from a friend-friend. We'll define the different types of business relationships in the next chapter, but right now, know that these are not deep-dark-secrets, shoulder-to-cry-on relationships, more like we-can-laugh-together-in-the-breakroom bonds.) They don't need to know your life story, but you want them to be able to say "Oh, Lauren? She's a team player. She's easy and pleasant to work with. She has her shit together." Your colleagues will feel like they know you once they've chatted with you about pop culture or your kids or your recent vacation. Or, alternatively, once they've chatted with you about work over drinks outside of the office.

The irony of this concept—this idea that your colleagues might not "know" you—is that, when you're the only person of color, or one of very few, everyone knows you. They may not know your name, or they might always pronounce it wrong, but you already stand out. There is no avoiding being known, because you have nowhere to hide.

But no one is ever going to say "Sure, I know Lauren, she's the Black woman who sits two desks over from me." At least they won't say it publicly. And if they can't speak to your personality or what it's like to interact with you, if they can't point to specific work products and wins, they will default to "I don't really know her."

So really, the question you need to ask yourself once you've settled into a job is not "Are you known?" The question should really be "What are you known *for*?" Because you want to be known for more than just being the Black Person or the Other Latina. You want to be known for the fact that you're a good colleague and for all the great work you do. That is the reputation that will get you ahead.

Your Reputation Precedes You

When we talk about being known in the workplace, what we're really talking about is reputation. When I was in my first job, it wasn't that I had a bad rep. I had *no* rep. I wanted to be successful, so I worked hard, but I also had a 90-minute commute to and from work each day. I didn't want to kick back with my co-workers because I was on a schedule. Women of color often take this approach, coming into professional roles with reservation, or with our guard up, because that approach was ingrained in us or because the pressure of being the first or the only is so great. It takes time to warm up to colleagues, to get friendly, and to feel comfortable. Sometimes it is not inherently in us and at times it takes more effort. Sometimes we're looking not at the long game of connection, but at the short game of standard pleasantries, doing the work, and going home. I know, I was once there.

But this approach doesn't work in today's workplace. It's not enough to just *be* good at your job. Your colleagues and higher-ups—and specifically the right colleagues and higher-ups—need to *know* you're good at your job; otherwise you're operating in a bubble.

And listen, that might be fine with some people! There are, absolutely, workers who are fine with doing good work and going home. They work in their bubble and they do good work, but they don't get promoted and they don't get a raise. There's a lot of conversation about quiet quitters these days—people doing the bare minimum just to collect a paycheck—but I guarantee that is hurting the next generation of leaders. And for women of color, who already have so many extra obstacles stacked against them, it makes me especially worried. You're trying to quietly quit? Well, you might quietly get fired. But I know that's not actually *you*, because you picked up this book.

So much of success is reliant on the influence of other people. I would guess that probably 85 percent of the workplace decisions that will directly affect you are being made when you are not in the room. This is true internally, at your current job, but also externally, at other potential companies and among players in your industry as a whole. Internally, people are talking and asking themselves, *Who is going to lead this part of the business? Who is going to run point on this project? Who can we trust to interface with this client?* Yes, sure, sometimes you're in a meeting and your boss will ask for volunteers (and better raise your hand, but we'll get to that shortly), but more often than not your boss or manager is the one having this conversation with his or her colleagues. And similar conversations are taking place outside your specific place of business, whether a company is looking to recruit someone new, an industry conference needs a speaker, or an organization is putting together the invite list for their annual holiday party. In all of these situations, you not only want your name to come up, but also to come up quickly. Decisions are made in an instant. People are so time-strapped that whoever they think of first, that's who's going to get the call.

So how do you make sure the right people have a positive opinion about who you are? You have to take a two-pronged approach: personal and professional. You have to make connections, and you have to have wins.

Connections, Not Contacts

Let me be clear: there's a big difference between connecting with people and meeting people. Connections are relationships. They're made over time. You can gather an entire Excel grid of contacts, but then what? What can you do with that list? Can you call on them when you need a reference? Can you ask them for a favor? And would they do those things for you? Probably not. What you have with that contact list is just that—a list of people you know. Great. What you want instead are people you can call on when necessary, and who feel safe to do the same with you. Connection, after all, goes both ways.

But let's start at the beginning. How are you going to connect with people in the first place? By the time I started my second job at the global PR firm, the one thing I knew for certain was that if I wanted to prioritize relationships within the company, I was going to have to be proactive. I couldn't wait for invitations. Maybe someone would say "Let's include Lauren" in a meeting or outing, but I knew better than to rely on that. And so I raised my hand to be on committees. I showed up to the after-work happy hours. I chatted with my peers and popped by their desks to say hi. If there was a team outing, you can be sure I signed up. These are the places where relationships are made. They aren't happening in the conference room or on the Zoom meeting, because once you sit down at that table, it's all business.

I don't want to pretend like everything was perfect at this next job just because I went to a happy hour or two. The truth is, I was often asked to be the one to get coffee or take notes. And I was not the best note-taker. It was not my specialty. I asked to be on the holiday committee and was told it was full, though I knew that there was not a single person of color in the group. This was especially annoying because I also knew that's where the important conversations were taking place. (Why was the holiday committee such a hotbed of power? Beats me. But I paid enough attention to know that's where the information was shared.) It was frustrating, discouraging, and—when it came to the coffee—downright insulting, but with all those noes there were also some yeses, and I took every one of those yeses and ran with it as best I could.

As a junior or midlevel employee, making connections outside your organization is just as important as doing so inside. The days of joining one company at the beginning of your career and staying there for decades are long gone. It happens, but it's rare. Studies show that the average worker will hold 12 different jobs in their lifetime.[1] If you're looking to move up the ranks in any given industry, you'll need to make connections across different companies and across levels. You never know where your next big break will come from, which means that your networking can't be relegated to nine-to-five (as if nine-to-five hours even exist anymore). You will need to join professional organizations and attend conferences or summits. You will need to reach out to people on LinkedIn. The old practice of going to a networking event and exchanging business cards isn't as prominent as it once was, but if that opportunity comes up, yes, take that, too!

Connections, of course, will look different depending on the person on the other end. You can stop by your peer's desk to chat, but you can't show up unannounced at the office of a senior leader. And yet, having the support of someone at the executive level—or at least being on their radar—can be a major difference-maker to your future at a company. This is where wins come in. Your higher-ups are more likely to take an interest in you, and carve out time for you, if you've proven that you can execute. We'll talk about that in a minute, but for now let's say you've got the credibility. You've had some successes in the workplace that you can point to, which means you've probably been at your company for at least three to six months already. Now let's say there's a specific senior leader you would like to connect with—either because you've heard they're the key player, or because you think they have a lot to teach you, or because you think they could be a good advocate for you going forward. Your first plan of attack should be to try to at least say hello to this person at the next company-wide event. (I use the phrase "plan of attack" figuratively. Try to play it cool. Do not hover, and do not move in too quickly and pounce on a leader who's just trying to get a bite to eat.) Introduce yourself, and be ready to say something concise but of substance—maybe reference a project they led that you admired, or mention that you're interested in learning more about their area of the business. If that's too hard (and it might be, because the more senior the leader, the less likely you'll be to see them hanging around a company shindig), send them an e-mail introducing yourself and dropping whatever substantive nugget you might have said in person. Again, this is presuming you've got the work product to back it up, but given that, it's time to show initiative.

Now, be forewarned: if and when you e-mail someone two or more levels above you, people will be shocked. They'll say, "I can't believe you talked to the SVP of XYZ!" Your manager might say, "Why didn't you go through me?" If you mention your intention beforehand, they'll say, "Don't reach out, I'll make sure to connect you." Everyone is trying to manage up, and supervisors often like to control the chain of command—specifically to be sure they've got their people on lock, and that no one is going over their head. Even if you don't let your manager know what you're up to, or if you never volunteer that you're reaching out to a senior leader, 95 percent of the time it will get back to them. I'm not saying you need your manager's approval to ask someone else for advice; I just want you to be prepared for the fact that they will find out. (If there's one thing I hope this book will protect you from, it's being caught by surprise at work.) Now let's say you tell your boss that you'd love to connect with the head of the department, and he or she says, "No problem, I'll send an e-mail connecting you." Here's the thing: sometimes they'll follow through, and sometimes they won't. Ultimately it will come down to what best serves them. Not because your boss is some sort of evil manipulator, but because at the end of the day everyone at the office is looking out for themselves. Which of course is what I want for you, too. You are responsible for your own career. You need to maximize your wins and set yourself up for success, and you can't put that very important work in the hands of somebody else. Frankly, it would be careless to work somewhere and *not* put in the effort to get the most growth out of that environment. Too often as people of color we wait for our superiors to come to us and tell us, *You are going to get promoted! You are getting a raise! You are getting a new project!* All of these are things you have to go after, and connections are no different. When you're in the minority group in an office, it's rare that someone in the majority group will seek you out just to get to know you. Connections, like everything in the office, are not handed to us without effort.

That said, there is a difference between going after a connection and feeling entitled to it. If you are a junior to midlevel employee asking for a senior leader's time, you have to respect the food chain. You are asking something of someone whose time, at least in terms of the company, is more valuable. That doesn't mean you shouldn't ask for it, just that you need to be cognizant of what you're asking for and be clear about that understanding. Don't request an hour of this person's time or recommend that you go out to lunch. Start by asking for a 15-minute phone call, something that doesn't require them to go very far out of their way. (But please, do not just say, "Whenever works for you!" and expect this call will happen. "Whenever works for you" puts the responsibility on the other person to look through their massive calendar and choose a time slot for something that they may not particularly care about doing. "Whenever works for you" is the quickest way to ensure that you never actually meet with someone. Suggest some times. If you say, "Would eleven A.M. on September twenty work for you?" it will force them to be specific in their answer. They will be much more likely to respond and say "Eleven A.M. doesn't work, but I could do three." Then, voila, you've got your meeting.) And if you are granted that, you need to be ready with specific questions or specific information you want to share when those 15 minutes start. Choose questions that show you already know about the work they are doing, or that you want to be collaborative. *I see that you brought in X business; how did you land that? I see that you are leading Y project; is there anything I can do to help?* If you are struggling in a certain area, tell them about it and ask for some advice. You want to ask questions that provoke an actionable answer, rather than just a sermon. Do not just ask someone for their story. Nobody wants to spend time telling you "their story." They *do* want to spend time helping you navigate a challenge to find a solution, because that makes them feel useful and valued.

Here's the other thing about the dreaded "tell me your story" request: if this is someone relatively high up, you should be able to find their story online. Don't ask someone to give you information you should have been able to find on your own. Do your research and show up prepared. Skipping this basic Google search is a pretty clear indicator that you are interested in this person not because of who they are so much as in the title they hold. Just because someone five levels above you at your company has a fancy title or an executive role, they are still a person. They want to know that you chose them for a reason—maybe you see your future self in them, or you connect with the story they already shared in an interview or on a podcast. No one wants to feel like "You have ten executives to meet and are filling a quota and I'm the fool that spent time talking to you." Even if that's what you're doing, you should come to each meeting as if it's your only one. In my role at ColorComm, I've had people reach out to me and ask to connect, and then they say something like "Why did you start ColorComm?" That information is all over the Internet, so I take it as an immediate red flag. It begs the question *If you didn't do your homework on me, why should I invest in you?* (It's the same thing with job interviews. When we interview candidates at ColorComm, our director of operations will often ask, "What do you know about the company? Why do you want to work here?" I swear, you'd be shocked at how often people say, "I actually haven't done much research; I don't know much." Why would we continue with the interview process if you haven't done any research?)

With any connection, it's important to remember that meeting someone one time is just that, a meeting. Making a connection takes time, and it requires more than a single interaction. Which brings me to your followup. When you meet someone new, especially if it's an individual outside your organization or a higher-up on the corporate ladder, you need to follow up. Whether it's a "Nice to meet you" or a "Thank you for your time," the onus is on you to maintain the relationship and to be proactive in the follow-up process. It's also the first step toward securing that second meeting. But the timing here is critical. If you meet someone in person at a networking event or some other professional outing, I do not recommend reaching out the very next day. That's too much! Chances are, whoever you met also met at least five other people, and they don't want an onslaught of e-mails the next day. Let the interaction marinate. Give it time and space and then, maybe 7 to 10 days later, follow up.

Of course, before you write that e-mail (and please make it an e-mail—this is business; do not text them), take a moment to consider: What are you following up *with*? Well, let's revisit the question that I hope will drive your career: What do you need? Maybe all you need is the connection. You don't have a specific ask, but you know this relationship might be beneficial in the future. Great. In that case, your followup can be short and sweet. *Great meeting you; wanted to shoot over my info so you have it. I look forward to keeping in touch.* Maybe you include a sentence or two about what you do, both as a reminder and also to help them consider what they might need from *you* one day. Every connection should be mutually beneficial.

If you do have an ask, keep it brief. Don't follow up with a novel. Be specific, and stick to one paragraph, two at most. And if you really don't know the person all that well, schedule a call. This will allow them to ask questions and get all the information they need without an annoying back and forth. Maybe all you need is to say, "Let's do it again soon!" But think long and hard before you ask a favor of someone you've just met. If you are inviting them to speak somewhere and there is a benefit to them, okay, consider it. But beware of asking favors of people you haven't earned any relationship cred with. It's not a great look.

One quick word of caution when it comes to connections: Your reach should be wide, not necessarily deep. You don't need to have long, soulful conversations with everyone. This is not dating. You can have meaningful work connections without ever meeting that person's family or their significant other. I say this because it's more important to create a large number of strong-enough connections than a single superdeep one. Those may come, in time. But honestly, it's fine if they don't. It's tempting, if you've met someone with whom you hit it off, to think, *Whew, okay, I did it! I've made my connection, we've got each other's backs, now I'm going home.* But here's the thing. One is never enough. One person can quit in an instant, and then where are you? I had a friend in D.C. who got his first job through a connection of his uncle, who was a top client of his employer. It was worth it to that company to hire my friend to keep the uncle happy, and that bought him safety for a couple of years. But then his uncle retired and my friend's job security was finite, and once his uncle left, he was pushed out. No single connection, no matter how strong or how influential, is enough.

Carla Harris, former vice chairman of Morgan Stanley, once said that relationships are built on the number of touchpoints you have with someone. In other words, the work of connecting is never done, but it does get easier. When you first meet someone—whether it's someone outside your company, someone internally who's in a different department, or a senior-level executive with whom you wouldn't otherwise cross paths—you should drop them a line once a month or so to keep the relationship going. Once it's more established, your touchpoints won't have to be so frequent. Maybe once a quarter you'll send a quick note saying that you're thinking about them. Maybe every six months. Time really does go by quickly as your career builds. At this point, there are people I haven't spoken to in years that I would feel comfortable asking for 20 minutes of their time if I really needed it, but that's because I spent years nurturing our professional connection. When it comes to relationship building, you want to be playing the long game.

Wins

There are two different reasons why people might want to get to know you, and eventually vouch for you. The first is the personal stuff—maybe you and a peer have shared a laugh at a happy hour or have a mutual love of running; maybe a higher-up sees herself in you, or you've taken the initiative and shown an interest in her work. The second reason is on the professional side—you've had successes in the workplace that have established you as someone people want to learn more about. Often these two pieces go hand in hand. If someone feels connected to you, they want to help you get some wins. I've had instances where the people around me were doing similar work, getting similar pats on the back, and yet they were moving up and I wasn't, because I hadn't made strong connections. On the other hand, everyone is so strapped for time these days, and people are so determined to use every second wisely, that they're unlikely to invest in connecting with someone until that person has proven they can deliver. This is why it's so important that you have wins. Tangible successes give you credibility, and create a reason for people to seek you out for connection.

In today's office, every one of us is our own brand. And like any brand, you can have a great product, but if nobody knows about it, it's just sitting on the shelves. As you proceed through your career, I want you to keep this in mind. You want to be sure your colleagues know you, but more specifically, you want to be sure they know what you want them to know. How do you ensure that the people in your professional orbit know your strengths, your skills, your wins? That is what will separate you from the pack. Yes, you want your colleagues and superiors to know that you're a person, not just a number, but come promotion time, that's not enough. It might be enough to save you from the jaws of the "cultural fit" excuse, but it's not enough to get you the raise or promotion that you so likely deserve.

Becoming known for your wins is a multistep process. First, of course, you need to have the wins. You can't fake victories. But once you have those wins, you need to be sure the right people are aware of them. Oftentimes in a workplace, this is the hardest part. Ensuring that the right people in the right rooms know what you've achieved involves being strategic about who you connect with and how. It's not just a matter of shouting your achievements with a bullhorn. Wouldn't that be nice? But no, like everything in office politics, self-promotion is a much more delicate dance.

Like I said, before you can promote your wins, you need to be sure you have some wins to promote. As CEO of my own company, I've seen it happen too many times that an employee comes skipping into my office, excited to tell me about today's big victory. "Great!" I say. "What happened?" Then she goes on to tell me she's accomplished something that, sorry to say, I thought was a basic expectation. Doing what is asked of you, even if you've never done it before or you had to go out of your comfort zone to do it—that is not a win. That is something your hiring manager assumed you could do, which is why the company offered you the job. So before you start tooting your own horn, make sure you are clear on how your company defines success. Ask your boss on day one, so that you're sure you are aligned: *What does success look like to you? What are some wins you would like to see?* If you work in communications and you're trying to get your client a media hit, getting them placed in a local Iowa newspaper is very different from a full spread in *Vogue*. If you're super excited because you did something required of you that you've never done before? Awesome. Call your mom and tell her. Brag to your best friend. But be careful about broadcasting it widely if it's a baseline expectation, because that can backfire on you, making you seem immature or in over your head.

This doesn't mean you need to land a giant client out of the gate. Eventually, sure, you might want to be known for bringing millions of dollars of revenue to your company, for successfully leading teams, for increasing productivity by 25 percent. But that's not going to happen from the jump, and no one expects it to. Start small. What is something your boss recently commented on or gave you accolades for? Is there a project you worked on that had a great outcome? You don't have to have been the project manager to have contributed to its success. Your wins can also be more personnel related—maybe you are a team player, which can pay off because more people choose you for their projects, or you've taken on leadership roles for smaller projects or committees. If this is what the people around you are taking notice of, great. As long as you can point to your own success, you can start small and achieve greatness over time. Because once you are killing it in a small capacity, you will be invited to do more.

When I first started working at the global PR firm, I was good at writing press releases and securing media hits. It wasn't groundbreaking, but it was enough of a strength that I was eventually entrusted to start working with the top-tier, high-profile media companies. Over time, I secured a couple big-time placements—I got clients on *MSNBC* and a profile piece in *The Washington Post*. I had the wins, so I set out to be sure I was known for those achievements.

Which begs the question: How do we make sure that people—and the right people at that—know about all the good work we've done? Well, it starts with patience. Getting a win at the office can be a huge rush. I've been there—there's a buzz that comes from pulling off a major accomplishment that is hard to ignore. But you can't immediately go running to your boss's office and shoving it in their face. Before you go asking for accolades, give your manager a minute. Allow them some time to give you that pat on the back. If they haven't said anything after a week or maybe 10 days, then you should absolutely let them know. Tie it back to your conversation about what defines a win. "Per our chat, you mentioned a win looks like [THIS]. I was able to deliver recently, with [THIS WIN] and I wanted to check in and make sure the process was satisfactory." Everything should be positioned as a learning experience.

But it's not just your boss who needs to know about your accomplishments. If there's one thing I've learned about business as time has passed, it's that you need to think holistically. Any single person can leave a company or keep information to themselves. You want to be sure decision-makers know about your successes, and also people on other teams or in other departments. If your manager does eventually e-mail you some kudos, keep a record. You can always forward that to a senior leader—once you've already made the initial connection—and say something like, "I'd love your advice on how to collect more similar wins." Same goes for looping in other departments or even folks who are below you in the corporate structure. Maybe you couch the information around how you can partner on similar projects in the future. The key is self-advocacy, because if you've had a major accomplishment, folks may never know unless you tell them. I know this can sound intimidating—women of color often hesitate to promote their own accomplishments for fear of appearing bold or cocky—but because we often work in spaces where few people look like us, we are often our only advocates.

Now, a caveat: it's important to remember that broadcasting your wins is not a practice of shouting from the rooftops. When I had those successful media placements, I took them to the higher-ups who did similar work and who I wanted to learn from or work with. "I was recently able to secure a *New York Times* placement for our client, and I was wondering if I could work with you on *USA Today*," I said. Maybe for you that looks like "I was able to secure *X* client, and I would love to work on *Y* piece of business." But it needs to be purpose-driven, especially if you are talking to someone higher up in your company. The message they should receive is: "I'm sharing my wins in hopes of helping you achieve your goals." It's not about yelling, "Look at me!" and cheerleading for yourself, because that probably won't be received well. Everyone has wins, and if everyone took turns broadcasting them over a loudspeaker, just for the thrill of the applause, no one would ever get any work done.

Remember how I mentioned that you should have wins under your belt before reaching out to senior leaders?

In general, I think you should wait to e-mail anyone in a fairly senior role until you've been at the company for at least three months (that is, assuming you aren't in a senior role yourself). Between meeting your direct colleagues and getting settled into the workflow and learning company processes, it's hard to have any major wins before 90 days. But also, during your first 90 days, everyone at the company is evaluating you. You don't want to seem as if you're more focused on climbing the ladder than on doing your job, which is why I generally suggest only reaching out to your peer group during that early orientation period. But also, leaders may not want to offer their time until they know that the person they're giving that time to has a future at the company. People leave organizations at a rapid rate, and no one wants to invest in someone who could leave the next day. There's also that pesky manager problem. As I said, some managers will think it's inappropriate for you to reach out to a senior leader on your own. You can only concern yourself with that so much, *but* if you are going to get your hand slapped for going around your manager, you want to do it with some wins under your belt. Wins buy you safety—it's hard for a manager to complain about a high-performing employee who wants to learn and grow. But if you have no successes in your portfolio, it's easy to create a narrative about an employee focusing her energy in all the wrong places.

Another important thing about wins: they inspire curiosity from others. Once you're successful, people want to know more about your habits—they want to understand what you're doing differently, and what's driving your accomplishments. Do you read a lot? Do you work out? Are you an early riser or a night owl? Where did you learn to pitch that client or speak that language? Suddenly all the pieces of your life that make you a well-rounded human and not just a worker become more interesting to the people around you. Now these habits or hobbies are a window into your accomplishments, and everyone wants to see the view.

At the end of the day, wins are an important ingredient in getting to know people because work is ultimately about the bottom line. Can you perform? Are you a good investment for the company? Are you easy to work with? In the quest to get more money and better titles, all of that still comes before whether we shop at the same places or eat at the same restaurants. And if you do, even better. Connection + wins = good reputation.

Getting Noticed

Connections and wins are both long-term strategies. They are the most powerful in terms of building social capital, but they should be supplemented with some quick-hit behaviors that, when practiced consistently, will ensure that people notice you.

Speak up. You should make your voice heard in meetings, but when you speak, add value. Be thoughtful every time you open your mouth. Saying "I agree" or starting a sentence with "Just to clarify" do not count. Don't echo what someone else said just to hear yourself speak. You need to provide insight to where colleagues will say, "That's a good idea," or "Let's consider your point of view." If you're in the minority group in an office, it's likely you'll be able to offer perspective that *is* different. You'll have different cultural reference points and a different upbringing, and that will hopefully translate to helping your team see things from a new point of view. Another meaningful and important contribution is speaking up if there is cause for concern. Sometimes women of color can spot problematic content where others—men, white colleagues—cannot. If you get feedback that sounds like "Let's consider what Lauren just said," that will signal that you added value. You contributed meaningfully. If you make a comment and you're met with crickets, that's a sign you didn't resonate with anybody.

Be consistent. You do not need to speak every single time your colleagues gather in a room, but it does have to happen more often than not. One bright idea can be written off as a fluke, but no one can deny the person who always has something valuable to add. Plus, multiple people are present at each meeting, so the more you contribute, the more people can attest to your added value. Being "known for" something is about multiple people having the same impression.

Join, join, join. When it comes to joining internal groups, it's important for you to think about variety. Chances are you already know the other employees of color because there aren't that many of you. The goal of joining groups is to get to know as many people as possible, because it's important that people across ages, races, genders, and departments know that you're really funny or a problem-solver or a great team player. Joining groups also shows a high level of engagement in company culture, which will help you get integrated into the company itself. As for external groups, this is how you learn about your industry and how your industry learns about you. One important note here: a lot of industry groups or networking organizations cost money, and your company won't always pay for you. I always suggest that junior and midlevel workers set aside professional development funds as part of their personal budget. We invest in everything else: vacations, clothes, gifts, family. Your career should be just as important. If you want to have a long professional journey, you can't always say, "My company isn't investing in me so I can't afford to join." At ColorComm, I see the members who pay and the members who are getting a free membership from their company, and, frankly, people are more invested when they pay for themselves. It's bigger than the dues; you are investing in your future. It is an investment in yourself, and you are absolutely worth it.

— 3 —

YOU NEED . . .
TO ACTIVATE YOUR
NETWORK

When ColorComm celebrated its 10th anniversary in 2021, I had one dream guest: Michelle Obama. *It would be so powerful*, I thought, *if she joined us to celebrate this network for women of color and all we had accomplished.* I don't have a personal connection to the former First Lady, but I knew several people who had worked with her in the past. One of those people was Deesha, a professional friend who served as the White House Social Secretary under President Barack Obama. Deesha and I hadn't spoken since before the pandemic—you know how that time was, with people hunkered down, big work events sidelined, networking on hold. So it had been about two years with no conversation between us aside from the occasional Instagram messages. However, in the years before the pandemic, back when we were both coming up in our respective careers, we had put effort into building our relationship. We'd had lunch, we shared mutual friends, we'd chat whenever we crossed paths at professional functions. I had enough confidence in the professional relationship that I didn't think twice about e-mailing her as I tried to understand how to go about relaying the Obama invitation.

I e-mailed Deesha and made my ask. *We'd love to have Mrs. Obama join as a guest,* I wrote. *We have Whoopi Goldberg joining already and Valerie Jarrett.* Deesha wrote back immediately and said, *Give me a call when you have a moment today.* Barely a word between us in two years and she was willing to get on the phone with me that afternoon.

This is the power of an activated network. Not all connections are created equal. Knowing a lot of people is great, especially in the early days of your career journey, but as your professional star rises your focus should shift to knowing *the right* people. If making a name for yourself is level one of the networking game, activating your network is level two. When you first start out in the working world, knowing people is almost a protective measure—it can help you settle into your job, or find a place in your company. But over time, you want to be thoughtful about building a network that is set up to serve you in the long haul and where you can also contribute.

Deesha and I spoke on the phone that same day, and she happily told me the people I needed to connect with to extend the invitation to the former First Lady. Deesha shared those people's contact information and gave me permission to use her name in the note (as in, "Deesha suggested I reach out to you.") There will come a time in your career when your name has currency, and you won't offer it up unless you're confident the person using it won't make you look bad. That Deesha granted me that privilege showed professional trust. In the end, Mrs. Obama couldn't attend our luncheon, but she wrote an open letter to ColorComm, and we invited her comms director to read it for the group. It was phenomenal! We felt her presence in the room, she spoke to the value of our organization, and to me it was a "big win."

When your career is just starting out, making connections is about meeting people and learning from them. Activating your network comes when you've already put in the work to cultivate connections and now you need to ensure you have the right mix of people in your corner—people who will go to bat for you, and for whom you will do the same. With an activated network, you can find the appropriate contact for whatever circumstance you find yourself in, whether you need an introduction at a different company, information about how to join a professional organization, or whatever else. You need more than a circle of passive relationships, even if those relationships are very warm or friendly.

Years ago, a new member of ColorComm said she wanted to quit after only being a member for one month. The membership team asked her why she wanted to leave and she said she hadn't gotten anything out of it. So they asked: Have you participated in events? Did you connect with the board? Did you sign up for the mentorship program? To each question this woman answered, "No, I haven't had time." All the opportunities were there for her, but she had to be the one to make something happen—activating a network doesn't happen by magic. You need to put action behind it. When I talk about activating your network, I'm talking about harnessing the power of the relationships you've cultivated, which must be authentic and intentional for them to grow.

Evaluating the Holes

Networks, as we've noted, are ever-changing. The professional world is more of a revolving door today than it has ever been. People come and go at a rapid rate. And they don't just move between companies. They jump from one industry into a completely different one. They leave corporate America to start their own gig. Their side hustle becomes their main hustle. They leave the workforce entirely. All of this is why it's so important to continually evaluate the holes in your network, and it starts, once again, with understanding what you need. Do you need advice on how to ask for a raise? Do you need help choosing which professional organizations to join, or insight into who are the most respected people in your industry? Do you need an introduction? Do you need to know who you need to know? Once you can articulate what you need, you can assess your current network. If there's no one who can help you fulfill a particular need, then the hole in your network is obvious.

Let me be clear, this all takes a lot of work. I know that firsthand. But as women of color we have to be intentional about building the *right* network, because we're much less likely to have been born into it than our white counterparts. Experts estimate that up to 80 percent of professional workers—80 percent!—get their jobs through networks. Some estimates say that up to 70 percent of jobs are never even posted on job sites—they are filled by word of mouth before they are even posted.[1] And yet, a 2018 study found that women of color are 35 percent less likely to get job referrals than white men.[2] Not exactly an even playing field, as we already know. But it's not just about getting jobs. It's about getting information. There's been increasing attention paid recently to what's being referred to as "the network gap," the advantage that some people have over others as a result of who they know. Research shows that where you grew up, where you went to school, and even where you work currently can give you up to a 12-times advantage in gaining access to opportunity. Which is to say, if you weren't handed professional connections by your parents or your neighborhood or your boarding school alumni network, you need to build them on your own.

And again, it's a big undertaking. I know that because I did it, too. As my career grew, I got savvier about connections. I got involved in the Spelman alumnae organization, and it was the people in that network who said to me, "You need to know Tara Jones." At the time, Tara Jones was the VP of communications at BET, and she was a fellow Spelman alumna. Once we connected and I began to tell her my professional goals, her wheels started spinning, and she suggested a handful of other people I should know. Tara ended up being the keynote speaker at the very first ColorComm luncheon, and a number of those other "you should know" individuals were in attendance or spoke at later events. That's how it works. But it doesn't happen overnight, and it doesn't come easy.

Gathering Valuable Intel

The trickiest part about evaluating the holes in your network and making sure you've connected with the right people is that often you don't know who the *right* people are. Once I learned the importance of connections and realized that I was going to have to seek them out, I made a conscious effort to identify people I wanted to know—people who were getting awards; people on panels; people whose names came up in articles about my industry. These were people I already knew had clout and connections and knowledge I could benefit from, so I reached out to them on LinkedIn or tried to attend conferences or events where they might be speaking. It worked, but it took effort.

Of course, you'll also meet many individuals over the course of your professional career in less deliberate ways, and many of those people can become important contacts down the line. But when you meet someone at a networking event, it's not so easy to know if that person has what you need, whether that's insight into an area where you are struggling or a connection point to a CEO. People don't walk around wearing signs that say, "I know so-and-so," or "Ask me about THIS." You will only learn that information by putting in time, asking questions, and doing your research.

Which brings us back to connection building and what might be considered the next step in your relationship-building journey, because to know if you have the right connections, I guess it's fair to say you have to *know* your connections. Again, that doesn't mean you need long, intimate conversations. You also shouldn't be conducting an inquisition. Getting to know a professional contact is a gradual process over the course of about seven meetings or interactions. A person is not going to share everything (or everyone) they know the first time they chat with you. Start by taking a genuine interest in getting to know them. During your first one to three touchpoints, ask questions: Who are your mentors? Who do you mentor? Has anyone been instrumental in your career? What are some of your proudest wins, and how did you achieve them? What professional organizations have you been involved with, and have they been beneficial? These questions apply across the board, no matter the level of the person you are talking to.

And here's the thing: if you are truly interested in advancing in your own career, these are all questions that you should truly *want* to know the answers to. Relationships, even work relationships, shouldn't be strictly transactional. When we talk about being strategic with relationships or collecting contacts, it can sound disingenuous, but the truth is we can all tell the difference between being genuinely friendly with someone—and thus genuinely wanting to help that person out—and having a relationship that is entirely based on what you can do for each other. You want your connections to straddle that line. You want to be able to exchange pleasant banter or to inquire about their kids. If you are handling your interactions with emotional intelligence, then you can build a relationship that is mutually beneficial but also mutually fulfilling.

So let's say you've connected three times already, and you've begun to get to know each other. When it comes time for meetings four through seven, that's when more of an information exchange is going to happen. Instead of, or in addition to, learning about each other's work experience, you might be able to say, "Hey, I'm interested in joining the associate board of this organization; any chance you know anyone there?" or "I'd love to make a job change in the coming months, would you let me know if you hear of anything?" But you need to build up to that—you need to establish rapport. And think about it—seven interactions! If you're connecting with someone once every couple of months, those seven meetings could take a year. And honestly, work and life get so busy that once every couple of months might even be too ambitious. But the good news is, these seven-ish meetings will have a big return on investment. When you put the work in at the beginning, that mutual respect and appreciation for each other will stick, even as your touch-bases become less frequent. I hadn't talked to Deesha in a while, but we'd put the time in early, and it paid off.

As interested as you might be in gauging how someone can help you with your needs, you should be equally curious about how you can help them achieve theirs. Relationships are reciprocal. Yes, there are people who social climb or collect networks, but that's not what I'm advising. That will come back to bite you, believe me. I want you to focus on a give-and-take—even if you're not sure that this person *is* the right person for you, be open to finding out how you might be able to help them. After all, just because someone isn't the right contact for you today doesn't mean they won't be in the future. Your focus should be on a long-term, sustainable, substantive exchange. So ask this person what their goals are; tell them about your own mentors and connections, and any organizations you've been a part of. Maybe invite them to speak to an organization you're involved in—that way you're serving the person, you're serving the organization; there is value exchanged all around. Asking someone for a half hour of their time and then only trolling for information that will serve you is a one-way exchange. Make sure they know you see the two-way street.

I had a particular professional friend, and both of us were coming up in the industry. As our relationship progressed, she always seemed to ask me for things. I was happy to help, especially at the beginning. *You want a contact at NBC? At Disney? Sure, here you go!* I was rooting for her success—we were, I thought, rooting for each other's success. But over time things began to feel one-sided. I had put time, energy, and money into building my network, and I didn't get the sense that she did the same. What I saw was that she found a few people who had already done the work, and she asked for favors and was now acquiring her own networks off the backs of those who had done the work. Those are not connections, they are not professional friends. Those are users and moochers, and the moment either party realizes that they are doing all the giving and not getting anything in return, resentment will set in. Eventually, I stopped helping this woman out. I wasn't so quick to give out contacts that I had put effort into building. Like any relationship, the professional kind involve give-and-take.

The Right Mix

Activating your network is not only about knowing the right people, but also the right *mix* of people. Obviously that mix depends on where you work and what you do, but there are guidelines that apply regardless. To start, you want to know someone at every level of the corporate ladder. They don't all have to be at your company necessarily—this is about building an industry-wide network. Do you know an executive leader in your industry who you can call on to help you navigate a problem? Someone at the midlevel who can tell you about job openings? Someone at the junior level who can help you take the temperature of employees just starting out, or teach you what the newer members of the workforce are prioritizing in the office? I always say it's important for me to know someone in every decade of life. I need to have connections with people who are in their twenties all the way through their sixties because I want to understand how I can connect to audiences from 22 to 65, as ColorComm's member base is intergenerational. How will I know the best way to do that if I don't have relationships at each decade? The specifics of different jobs vary—reaching wide audiences might not matter to you— but it's always important to have access to different groups no matter what you do. If you're a graphic designer, you might want to be sure your work appeals to 20-somethings but can still be understood by 60-somethings. If you're in sales, you might need different tactics depending on who you're selling to. If you're in finance, your client's priorities will change depending on their age, and you need a way to get ahead of that.

The other reason for casting this wide net is simply that the workforce is always changing. Eventually the 60-something contacts will retire, and the 20-something contacts will move up. Before you know it, that junior-level employee you knew back in the day is running her own company, and thanks to years of building a relationship, you have an in. This happens all the time, which is why it's really not enough to know *a* person in each decade, you need to know a group of people in each decade.

Age diversity is one factor, but you want to think about diversity across the board. You should have strong connections with people who don't look like you, with every gender, with people in different industries or different subsections of the same industry. The more groups you can gather insight from, the better.

One Person Is Not a Network

I spoke in the previous chapter about the importance of pursuing multiple connections at a time. As you're making a name for yourself, this is critical because any one person can leave an industry or organization. A reputation is built on widespread beliefs about someone—one person does not make a reputation. But as you're considering how to activate your network, and really cultivating the relationships that you hope will serve you in the long run, this wide net becomes even more important. When I was early in my career, I would focus on building relationships with one person at a time. In one particular instance, I reached out to someone who was an SVP, and it took almost a year to get on her calendar. My first mistake was that I kept asking her to lunch. Lunch is great if both parties can see the mutual benefit to the relationship, but if the person you're trying to connect with is more senior than you, and they can't see how meeting you might help them (even if it might!), then interrupting their day for a lunch date is a low priority. Lunch outings are time-consuming! It's not just the hour in the restaurant, it's the commute to the restaurant and the buffer time at work before and after. When all is said and done, lunch can take two to three hours out of the workday. So know that if you ask for lunch, it definitely might happen, but it also might get rescheduled a million times. Getting seven(ish) meetings at this pace can take forever, and if you take a one-at-a-time approach, you'll never have that web of contacts you need to succeed.

The reality is, as much as we want our professional lives to build quickly, cultivating and activating a powerful network takes time. Aside from the time spent actually connecting, there's the time spent writing and sending e-mails and the time spent scheduling things in your calendar. There's the time spent researching who you might want to add to your "reach out to" list. You might keep a contact list (you probably should), and that requires upkeep. You might want to send a birthday note, or a congratulatory note when someone has a big achievement, which means paying attention to who is getting certain awards or being honored at certain events. All of which takes, yes, more time.

I think of all this as admin time. A lot of companies schedule in admin time—time dedicated to bringing in *new* business rather than time working on current business. You need to think of yourself as a company, and activating your network is akin to bringing in new business.

The right relationships will bring new revenue over time—through job opportunities or invitations or the right introduction—but this is why law firms, for example, foot the bill when their lawyers take clients or potential clients out to dinner. This work (and yes, it is work) pays off.

So how to fit these added tasks into your already full day? You have to schedule it, or it may never happen. I used to send myself calendar invites for "relationship-building time" so that I didn't forget. One of my mentors, an executive vice president of diversity at a major media company, told me that she schedules two hours, from 4 P.M. to 6 P.M. on Fridays, for this type of work. And this is an executive vice president! She has already climbed the corporate ladder, and it would be very easy for her to sit back and stop putting effort into relationships. But this work is never done. At this point, most of her admin time is dedicated to helping those who've requested her time—they want advice, they want to "pick her brain." In the immediate term, the conversations are a greater benefit to the person on the other end of the line than they are to her, but she still says yes and takes the calls when she can. Not only because they might benefit her in the long run (because they definitely might), but because by taking these calls she is helping the next generation of ambitious women of color. And ultimately that's what so much of this work is about. The more of us who know how to play the game and make our way to the top, the more space we can create for others who look like us.

The People We All Need

There's a lot of talk in the professional world about making sure you have a mentor or a sponsor, or about gathering your personal board of advisors. Each of these roles is different, and yet I find that ColorComm members—in fact, so many professionals I meet—are unclear on what differentiates one from another. So let me present you with this relationship glossary, the terms you need to know—and the people you need to embrace—as you activate your network: mentor, sponsor, businessship, godmother/godfather, and personal board of advisors.

Mentor

Of all the formalized professional relationships, mentor is the one that everyone is familiar with. And yet from the way I hear young employees throwing this word around, I get the sense that they don't always understand what this person actually does. So, please, pay attention.

A mentor is someone with whom you have an established relationship and who can help you in your career and provide guidance as you are climbing your career ladder. It's a relationship that is based on your career trajectory—they will give advice about your next steps (which job to apply for, which job to take, when it's time to move on, when it's appropriate to touch base with your boss) and help you navigate your professional journey. When you have a problem, you can go to your mentor and that person can help you come up with a solution. A mentor is someone who has already done whatever it is that you are trying to do. They've been through it, so they can help you see things through the lens of experience.

But please, take note of that definition again. A mentor is *someone with whom you have an established relationship*. Do not approach someone you have never met and ask them, explicitly, to be your mentor. (The only exception here is if your company has a formalized mentorship program and you have been tasked with recruiting your own mentor.) I cannot tell you how common this is. So much pressure is put these days on the importance of a mentor that junior-level employees often set their sights on someone without putting in the effort to build the relationship first. They write a note to someone they have never even met, or have barely met, and they think, because this person looks like them or went to the same college, that they will want to be their mentor. But here's the thing—a good mentor is going to put effort into a relationship. They are going to be invested in your success. To be a good mentor this person needs to *care* about your career, and why would someone who has never met you care about your career?

It's like dating. If you meet someone one time, you're not going to say, "Do you want to be in a relationship?" right away. That would be too much! It would scare the other person away! The same is true in the professional space. Once you identify someone who you believe could be a good mentor, start by connecting with that person in all the ways I've already described. Then let the relationship evolve over time.

The truth is, you never need to put a label on your mentorship. If you have a person in your network who is more senior than you, someone who is happy to answer your questions and guide you through work dilemmas, then you have a mentor. Ultimately a mentorship is just an ongoing conversation with someone who is older (if not necessarily in age, definitely in experience) and wiser. And sure, there are people who don't mind the label, but more often than not, people don't want to feel like they're a part of your master plan. Not to mention that asking someone to be your mentor can scare them off, because it sounds like a lot of work. When you're already invested in someone, the work of being a mentor comes naturally. But if you don't yet have a connection and you ask someone to be your mentor, they may just say no because they don't want to take on any extra work.

As a mentee, or a potential mentee, it's your job to drive the relationship forward, to be proactive, to reach out from time to time. Include touch-bases with your mentor in that "admin time" that I know you are scheduling in your calendar! (To be clear, and I hope I don't have to even say this, but if you are putting "connect with mentor" time on your calendar as a reminder to reach out, put it *only* on your calendar. Do not add these invites to your would-be mentor's already busy schedule.) Use the opportunity to send along an article you read that made you think of this person, or a note of congrats if they had a big achievement or if, for example, a board they are involved in had a success. Try to give them some information they might not be aware of. You might even suggest them for an award or honor. Something like, "I see that *Crain's* is taking nominations for their 40 Under 40 and I thought of you. I'd be happy to help with a submission." Remember, even mentors have areas where they have a lot to learn— with social media, perhaps, or new technologies. People think of mentorships as the older, more experienced colleague helping the junior colleague, but there have to be contributions from both sides in order to foster a strong mentorship that will follow you through your career.

Sponsor

A sponsor is someone who is not necessarily part of your day-to-day mentorship and guidance, but is still able to provide opportunities or to speak highly of your work.

They are happy to associate their name with yours because they know your output is good, so they vouch for you when opportunities come up or speak of you when you're not in the room. A sponsor might share your name for a speaking engagement. They might suggest you for the lead on a new client account or even for a potential promotion. They aren't helping you navigate the workplace or get to the place where they'd be willing to recommend you, but once you're fully baked and ready to do big things, they'll put your name forward and help you find those things.

The main difference between a mentor and a sponsor is that while a mentor is helping you "come up" in the industry, a sponsor says, "I know your experience, I've seen you produce wins, now let's get you the right opportunities."

Individual sponsor relationships are similar to sponsors at any large event. ColorComm throws a huge event every year, the ColorComm Conference, where we bring together hundreds of professionals, usually in a luxurious location, to discuss professional issues facing women of color. Like any large professional conference, we take on sponsors who are proud to associate their name with our production. Sponsors invest in your work, and they provide opportunity—in exchange for the shine of associating their brand with our good work. They choose to sponsor us largely based on reputation because they know we can achieve great things. Personal sponsors are just the same.

When you've found people in your professional network who you think could serve as sponsors, again, don't ask outright if they are willing to accept the role. This relationship doesn't have to be codified. You might say, "I'd be thrilled if you'd keep me in mind if any opportunities come up." A superior in your network might not know you are looking for opportunities until you spell it out. So this, yes, you can ask. But don't just say, "Will you be my sponsor?" Please, for the love of God, no.

Businessship

Your mentors and sponsors will likely have more career experience than you. That's why they have the wisdom and experience, and why their recommendations hold weight. When your sponsor recommends you for an opportunity, people listen because that person has already established power and credibility. A businessship, on the other hand, is a relationship between peers. It is a business friendship. You are usually at or around the same level, so you help each other out in the office and pass along opportunities when appropriate. It's a key connection, but it's also the one that people get confused about most often, because sometimes the lines get blurry.

Here's the thing about a businessship: It is not a friendship. You might run in the same circles, or have connections in common, but this person isn't showing up at the hospital if you hurt yourself. She's not coming to your rescue and listening to you cry after a breakup. A businessship isn't even the same as a work/office friendship, which is often predicated on venting or complaining about your boss or your workload or a new project. Work friends don't always have opportunities that they can include you on. Businessships, on the other hand, are fairly transactional. That might sound harsh, but it's important to be clear about the reality of the relationship or you can get burned. Yes, you enjoy each other's company, and you might have fun together at work functions, but that's where the waters can get muddy. It can look like a friendship and feel like a friendship, but in reality, it's not, and you can't have the same expectations of this person as you would your true ride-or-dies. You can't get mad at them when they don't show up at your birthday party, and they shouldn't get mad if you don't send a baby gift.

I've absolutely made the mistake of thinking that some of my businesships were actually friendships. It's not an unreasonable mistake. If you are someone who prioritizes her career and spends a lot of your "off" hours doing work-related activities (conferences, happy hours, events, etc.), you might spend more time with the colleagues with whom you share a businesship than you do with your own friends. And these relationships can be really fruitful. These are people who might put your name forward to join a committee that they are already on, or invite you as a plus-one to an industry event. They might send job opportunities your way or refer business to you if they don't have the bandwidth. And you will likely do the same for them. These are the transactions that make this relationship so powerful. The trouble comes if you start to have expectations, as if this person owes you something when of course they—like all of us—are looking out first for themselves.

I first found myself on the receiving end of these blurred lines in 2014, when I was invited to the Celebration of Design at the Obama White House. It was a fashion education summit—a gathering of some of the biggest heavyweights in the fashion industry. Vera Wang, Diane von Furstenberg, Anna Wintour, Jenna Lyons . . . It was a who's who of fashion and somehow I scored an invite, and I was so, so excited. I was supposed to be in Orlando for a conference, but I love fashion, and when the Obama White House calls, I say yes. I canceled my flight to Orlando so that I could attend. The next day, I posted about the event on social media, and a peer of mine—a stylist who worked in politics and with whom I had shared a businesship for a long time—reached out. "Why didn't you invite me?" she said. "You should have thought of me as your plus-one." The reality is that I didn't even have a plus-one, but honestly, when I got that invitation, I wasn't thinking of her. I was just excited to have made the list myself!

In businesships there will be times where you can pay opportunities forward, but it's not an obligation. It's a benefit. You don't owe anybody anything.

Godmother/Godfather

A professional godmother (or godfather) is someone who can point you in a direction that can save you 10 years. They can get you into rooms that you would otherwise never have access to. Professional godmothers are connected and respected, and they have power. These are the heavy hitters who are well known and can open doors for you with a wave of their proverbial wand. Of all the relationships I've mentioned thus far, this one is the toughest to come by. They are rare and take years to build, and if you have one, hold tight.

Professional godparents are not people you call on with regularity. You don't reach out every time you need advice. That is a mentor. The godparent is a back-pocket relationship; you only call on them when you could really use their help, but when you do, they actually pick up the phone. If you meet someone you think could be a godmother one day, play it cool. Do not ask them for anything out of the gate. Do nothing but show interest in them when you first connect. Eventually, if you play your cards right, this person will get a sense of your goals and, one day, out of nothing but an interest in giving you access, they'll invite you into a room that would otherwise be closed off to you.

Early in my ColorComm journey I had a godmother figure, Marcia. When the company was just starting out, I invited her to deliver the keynote at our D.C. launch party. She accepted, and shortly after, she asked me if I'd work a baby shower that she was throwing for another prominent woman in our industry. I was the attendant at this party—opening the door, greeting guests, making sure they had what they needed—but I was more than happy to serve in that role, because it put me behind closed doors with major players in my industry. I would never have gotten into that room on my own. At least not for another decade. Marcia was an incredible professional godmother, continually offering access to spaces that she knew would help me and my career.

When you are in a relationship like this, you may not be able to help this person professionally, but you should do what you can to reciprocate the kindnesses. Over the course of my relationship with Marcia, I sometimes helped with personal assistant–type matters like the baby shower, and I sometimes helped coordinate events when she needed an extra hand. I did these things pro bono, because so often compensation comes in forms other than money, and in this case, the relationship alone was of great value. I respected this person, I was grateful to her, and I wanted to be of service.

Personal Board of Advisors

This is a popular one these days. Everyone likes to talk about the importance of convening a personal board of advisors. Let me be very clear: these people do not meet.

Don't be fooled by the name. You do not gather them in a room or on a group text or mass e-mail when you need their help. A personal board of advisors is a group of 5 to 10 people who you can call on regularly for guidance. These are people who you trust to have your best interests at heart. That does not mean they are cheerleaders. They won't just say, "Yeah, you're doing great!" if you aren't. These are people who will challenge you when you need it and offer opportunity when you have earned it. The most important thing about your personal board of advisors is that the members are a diverse group—they don't all have to be in your industry and, in fact, you're better off if they're not. Your personal board of advisors should have different interests and different levels of experience. They might be people you've met during your personal time, at mom groups or church functions, or through sororities or fraternities. Maybe one has experience on a corporate board; maybe another works in finance and can help you understand how to grow and keep wealth. These are people who can help you navigate the corporate journey because you can't do this life alone. We cannot operate in a bubble and think we will succeed.

An important aspect of your personal board of advisors is that these people have been in the trenches. Even if they haven't worked in your specific industry, they have the professional experience necessary to give advice to help you get ahead. It can be tempting, I know, to think you don't need this group, because you have your family. *My family has my best interests at heart more than anyone*, you might be thinking. But very often, households of color don't have parents who have worked in these spaces. Workers of color are overrepresented in low-wage jobs; they are overrepresented in frontline industries like trucking, warehouse, the postal service, and home health care.

If the people in your family don't have experience navigating corporate environments, they may not be equipped to give advice that captures the soft skills and nuances that your career requires.

It's okay if reading about these different relationships makes you feel a little anxious. Building these kinds of professional connections often doesn't come naturally to women of color. We usually aren't born into these environments, which means we don't absorb these relationship skills by osmosis the way many of our white counterparts might. You might work in an office with colleagues whose networks have been activated since birth—their father might have a friend who's been waiting to pull strings for them since the day they were born. And that's not an exaggeration! It's all the more reason why we have to be strategic about creating access that will benefit us and benefit the companies we serve. For me, building and activating a network was a grassroots, one-on-one effort. And as I've mentioned, one of the biggest mistakes I made early on was focusing too much on cultivating a relationship with any single person. This is a common error: people think they need *one* mentor, *one* sponsor, and so on. Unfortunately, no. For each of these roles you need to think big— ideally you will start out with at least three to five people in mind for each role. That doesn't mean you will have five mentors and five sponsors or even five businesships, and you certainly will not have five godmothers. But especially with those mentors and sponsors, identifying and pursuing a number of potential relationships helps you increase your chances that a few will develop into something fruitful.

As you are doing all this work, don't forget that none of this is permanent. Your professional relationships will evolve and may not last forever. You may maintain the relationship, but, for example, what was once a mentorship could become a friendship. You might catch up professionally to where your mentor is, in pay or access or opportunity, and feel like you've outgrown the relationship in its current form. Maybe you had a sponsor or a godmother, and you used to be in the same room because they put you there, and now it's happening organically. Congratulations! You've caught up! I'm not going to lie to you, this can be awkward. Of course, the hope is that whoever was guiding you is thrilled that the little caterpillar they helped to nurture has now become a butterfly. The point of mentoring someone, after all, is to help that person get ahead. But these moments can also serve as a wake-up call to a mentor that things have shifted and changed, and that is not always a welcome change. People like to feel needed, so if you don't need your mentor/sponsor/etc. anymore, it can feel like a punch to the gut for that person. They might feel jealous or surprised or simply unprepared, and that can put a strain on your relationship. But this is part of your growth, and growth always comes with its own set of challenges.

If and when that time does come, it might mean you need a new slate of people to get you to the next step. You might need a new set of mentors to meet you where you are today. But it also might mean it's time for you to pay it forward. As important as it is for you to find role models and teachers, it's just as important to *be* a role model and teacher. There's power in these relationships, and when it comes to the workplace, we can use all the power we can get.

PART TWO

Establishing Your Position

— 4 —

YOU NEED . . .
TO KNOW YOUR
VALUE

Before I ran ColorComm full time, I worked as a communications strategist at a well-known crisis communications firm in Washington, D.C. One of the most critical
aspects of the work is observation. In order to best solve
a problem, you have to pay attention and ask questions:
What are people reacting to? What went wrong? What did
the client prioritize? What are their end goals? Managing
your career is similar. You have to pay attention to what's
important to the people around you and adjust accordingly.
Companies and bosses are constantly supplying information about what they value in their employees. They may
not tell you outright, but if you keep your eyes peeled and
your ears open, you'll learn what you need to know. At
this particular job, I noticed early on that the people in
charge really cared about the trade publication *PR Week*. It's
the bible of the public relations world, and senior leaders
within my division wanted to see their clients written up
in its pages. They talked about it all the time, so I started
reaching out to editors there and building relationships,
talking to them about clients and ColorComm and just

81

generally getting on their radar. When I relayed that information to my managers, they instantly became more interested in me. *Oh, you know editors at* PR Week*?* they'd ask. *Who? Could you connect us?* Suddenly, I'd become more valuable, both because I had positioned myself as someone who already "got it" *and* because I had relationships in my back pocket that they wanted to keep close.

When it comes to your career, being talented is an important thing, but it's not the only thing. The truth is, being good at your job doesn't necessarily equate to having influence at your company. We've been talking a lot about the importance of relationships and securing influential connections—with editors, with clients, with big names in your industry—as certainly a way to increase your value at an organization before you've ever increased its bottom line. But there are other value adds, too: Perhaps you have a deep archival knowledge of the organization, or you manage a group of dedicated employees. Maybe you're especially proactive about going after big accounts, or you've received noteworthy awards, or you volunteer with an outside organization that makes your company look good. It's important that you understand what you bring to the table other than your work product, and how those things might make you even more valuable to the company.

Anytime you're being assessed in the office, your company is looking at a number of different factors. The main one, absolutely, is clear: How is she contributing to our bottom line? If you're a big revenue driver, your job will likely be secure (barring any outrageous ethical missteps). But your managers are also evaluating you on other criteria: Is she adaptable? Is she a leader? Is she respected? Does she have connections or access that could help us drive our business forward? Is she a member of a country club or sorority that I want a connection to? Value is distributed across many boxes, and the more boxes you check, the more valuable you will be. And yes, value may translate into pay, but it might also correlate with inclusion, or ascension, or job security. If you are a revenue-producing employee who is awful to be around, your job will be safe, but you may not be invited to certain events or included in certain meetings or decisions. You will be looked at as work only, which doesn't translate to quick promotions or more influential roles. Nepotism or strong godmother relationships also have value—if you are the daughter of a top client, if you have a connection to Oprah or Hillary Clinton or Jennifer Lopez, you'll probably be kept around even if your work product doesn't warrant it. But if that's the only box you check, then you might be included on the social committees, but you won't be trusted with important projects or empowered to make decisions at an impactful level.

The Whole Package

As women of color, our value is often underestimated. On the most basic level, we can see it in our pay scale. As I mentioned in chapter 1, women of color—specifically Black and Hispanic women—make significantly less than our white counterparts. For every dollar a white man makes, a white woman makes 73 cents. But Black women make 67 cents, and Hispanic women make 54 cents. (And those cents add up! Research shows that the wage gap shortchanges Black women $22,692 per year and $907,680 over the span of a 40-year career.) There are also, of course, workplace biases that work against us, starting before we're even hired. Studies show that résumés with "distinctively

Black names" are about 10 percent less likely to be con-
tacted by employers regardless of the applicant's education, experience, or skills.[1] And this is especially true in
corporate America. In one study, researchers found that
the top 20 percent of the most profitable Fortune 500 companies accounted for about half of total instances of hiring
discrimination.[2]

In order to increase your value in the workplace, I
want you to continue to think of yourself as a brand. In
brand marketing, there's always a lot of talk about the halo
effect. It's about positive associations. The idea is that if a
brand has one great product, the halo around that product
will extend to other products by the same company. (The
increase in sales of Apple computers after the success of
the iPod is an often cited example.) The halo effect can
also extend to partnerships—if, say, an up-and-coming
brand partners with one that's highly regarded, the
up-and-comer will benefit as a result of the association.
But long before the halo effect was considered a marketing term, it was a psychological concept that applied to
individuals. In the most basic terms, people associate one
positive trait with another. The most popular example
of this unconscious bias is the assumption that someone
who is physically attractive must be a good person. But in
the workplace, it might be the assumption that someone
who is a good public speaker must be a good leader. Or
that someone with a good attitude has good work product. And there's a flip side to the psychological phenom-
enon—it's called the horns effect. This is another type of
unconscious bias, and it says that when we see one negative trait in someone, we'll extrapolate it to something
larger. We'll assume that someone who comes to work
dressed more causally must not be a good worker. Instinc-
tively, we, as women of color, already know this, even if

we didn't know the name for it. We were told from day one that we can't show up not adapting to our work environment because we can't give anyone an excuse to think less of our performance. And this effect has already been proven to hurt women of color in the workplace—if your characteristics stand out in a white-dominated space, they might be perceived negatively, and thus devalue the overall perception of you.

But if we go back to thinking of ourselves as a brand, we can make the halo effect work for us. The more "value added" boxes we check, the bigger our halo. You are probably already doing work, today, that is a value-add to your organization, so start taking stock. And think creatively! As women, we are too quick to sell ourselves short—studies show that we devalue our contributions when working on team projects with men,[3] we assess ourselves as having performed worse on tests (even when we actually scored the same),[4] and we charge less for our services than male counterparts.[5] We don't always consider the fact that whatever extras we're working on might have value to those who employ us. But every contribution counts for something, and if you don't have a full sense of what you're bringing to the table, how will anyone else? If you organize the annual boss's day celebration, if you participate in the company's mentorship program, if you organize lunch-and-learns, those are all value-adds. If people want you to speak at events, that's value, because it reflects well on your employer. If you have won a professional award, that means your company can brag about its award-winning staff. If you sit on professional boards or associate boards, your company might want to boast about its civic-minded employees. What if you've gotten professional certifications above what's required of you, and now your company can charge more for your time or service? It all counts.

It can be hard to keep track of your growing value as you rise. When I started climbing the professional ladder, I still thought of myself as that head-down timid employee who just wanted to do good work. I didn't give myself credit for how far I'd come. But by the time I had a year under my belt at the crisis communications firm, for example, my value had seriously increased. I continued to build ColorComm while I was employed there. Suddenly I wasn't just a communications strategist, I was a communications strategist who was doing important work to advance women of color in my industry. That made my company look good by association. And then I started winning awards and recognition for my ColorComm work (more on that later), and in every article it mentioned the company—halo effect! The company wasn't actually doing anything major to help women of color at the time, but because their employee was, they benefited. It took me too long to see how that external work could translate to internal value, so I'm here to save you some time.

The First, the Only, the Valuable

If you are reading this book, you might be the first woman of color in your position at your company. You might be the only woman of color on your team. You might be one of only a few women of color in your workplace. While these distinctions pose a whole host of challenges, they also add value—you are bringing something to your workplace that it very badly needs.

Being a first or only is a remarkable accomplishment. I don't want that fact to get buried in our discussion of how hard it is. It *is*, absolutely, hard. And exhausting. And frustrating. I know it, I've lived it. And it is a big responsibility, because while you might be the first, you don't want to be the last. But being a first, an only, or one of the few, is also something to be celebrated. You are breaking barriers. You are forging a path for the women of color who will come after you. But also, you are making your company look good. You look good to their stakeholders. You look good for their optics and PR. That's not to say it's why you are there—you brought skill or knowledge or experience or potential to the table, which is why they hired you. They could have gone with the status quo, the same hires they have made since the beginning of time. But the fact that you are a trailblazer reflects well on your company. You are making them look good, and it's important not to forget that, because that is value. That is influence.

Understanding the full value that you bring to a company is important for a lot of reasons—it adds credibility to your requests for a promotion or a raise, it builds clout with your higher-ups, and it helps you self-promote or sell yourself if you're looking for new opportunities. But it should also warrant extra support from your organization—if you and your success make them look good, then they should be helping to support that success. When it comes to being a first or an only, or even one of the few, it's important that your company sets you up with the resources necessary to achieve your goals. And, if they won't—if their promises to set you up for success turn out to be just lip service—it's important you find that out ASAP.

There will be times when companies make hires or promotions to check a box. They're getting pressure from outside and they want to make a quick change, so they execute a personnel shakeup as a Band-Aid measure rather than a true investment. They don't do it for a sustained, long-term, positive effect. If you recognize yourself in this scenario, it doesn't mean you're not qualified for your job.

Far from it. But it does mean that your company may not give you the resources required to do your job effectively. If you're put in a high-profile position and expected to create great change but you aren't given a budget or a strong team of workers reporting to you, how on earth can you be expected to do big things? What you need in this instance is important—you are making history, you are the first, all eyes are on you. You bring value as a change-maker. They need to recognize your value and match it with tools for making change.

A lot of leadership promotions that fit this bill happened in 2020 and 2021, when companies across the country were trying to act fast and diversify in the wake of George Floyd's murder and the subsequent racial reckoning. But personnel shakeups are not always specifically about race or for diversity optics. Research shows that women and workers of color are often promoted to leadership roles in times when an organization is in crisis or downturn. In these moments, companies believe they need to think differently, so they put leaders in place who represent a change of pace from the long line of white men who have come before. But being put in charge when things are struggling does not exactly make for an easy path to success. The problem is what's called the glass cliff: elevating women or workers of color into leadership positions when there's a giant mess to clean up. We inherit the role at a time when there's higher risk of failure—our hold on the top is precarious, and there's a long way to fall if things don't go well. Thus, the cliff.

If this is you, and you can tell early on that you are not going to get the resources or help you need—maybe you've been told there's no budget, or that you're reporting to someone who doesn't have any power within your organization—then you have to take a step back. It's hard, but this is when you say, "I'm not going to be successful in this role. I can't take it on just because it will help the company look good." Do not risk your own public failure for the company's sake. Yes, you should always bet on yourself, but you have to be realistic. After all, your company is looking out for itself. If you succeed, your supervisors look great. If you don't, the blame isn't theirs. So make sure you ask the important questions, and make clear what you need in order to be successful. And if you're met with stall tactics? If you ask what your budget is or what the reporting structure will look like or if you can bring in a new team and you're told, "We don't really know," or "We're not sure yet," or "We'll get back to you"? Well, then you have your answer. Companies are sure about everything else, so if they suddenly are unsure about this, then you are not going to get what you need to be successful in that role. You have value, and that value has power. Don't give it away without getting anything in return. Because the alternative is that you don't get what you need, you fail—how could you not?—and the company is not going to take responsibility. They are going to say, "We expected you to perform miracles with no resources, and you didn't do it." And then, behind closed doors, they'll say, "Welp, we tried—that's the last time we're going to take that chance. Just look at this example; she didn't work out, so let's go back to the status quo." You don't need that. Sometimes knowing your value means walking away and saying thanks, but no thanks.

It's What You Know *and* Who You Know

You already know that establishing relationships, especially the right relationships, will serve you throughout your career. The people you're connected with, if you've nurtured the relationships (and I know you have!), will give you advice, will make introductions, will send opportunities your way. But the deep list of connections you developed while finding your place is of value not only to you, but also to your company. Bringing connections to your organization can make you a deeply influential player—every connection is a potential client, collaborator, speaker, or partner, which translates to added revenue. When I made those editor connections at *PR Week*, it meant we had a better shot at getting our clients in the publication's pages, which meant we would look more successful in our clients' eyes. If you are a direct line to a specific person with influence or value to your company, that will make a difference to the powers that be.

But even when connections don't directly translate to an increase in the bottom line, the value-add is there. If you're not someone with one particular big-name connection, the fact that you are out there putting effort into building relationships will make a difference. (Most of us are not connected to household names, and it's not expected that you would be. That said, the higher you climb professionally, the more you *will* be expected to bring with you a list of connections that can translate to new business.) It's from networking and making connections that you might learn about new trends, or what business partnerships need to be developed, or who is looking for new work—all of which can affect a company's development and growth and ultimately its revenue. Companies need eyes and ears at industry events or other "extracurriculars"; they want information seekers, people whose webs of connections cross sectors. They want people who are excited to learn more about what is happening in their industry. This is true no matter what field you work in. Finance, media, marketing, law—they all have networking events. They have awards and panels. They all have engagements going on behind the scenes that expand beyond your day job. Companies don't want employees who just go to work and go home, so if you are out there networking, it's important that they know it. If you are the person known for putting in the time at spaces where you *could* meet the right people, even that potential is valuable, because you are someone who is constantly gathering information that will prove useful down the line.

While your network provides value in terms of making you more appealing and important to your employer, it also provides value in a form of protection, or insurance. Not all jobs work out, even for the most talented or most connected among us. If you know the right people, or if you have the ear of people all across your industry, your exit from a job where things aren't working out will be more pleasant all around. Your employer will treat you carefully rather than toss you aside. They will coddle you a bit, and maybe offer you a package when they otherwise wouldn't, because they know you have a line to important people and they are fearful of what could happen if the separation doesn't go well.

Of course, publicizing your network is an exercise in subtlety. Nobody likes a name-dropper. There's nothing more cringey than the person who says, "Do you know who I am connected to?" It's important that you spin any noteworthy connections as another way you might be able to serve your organization. If your company is looking for a speaker recommendation, maybe suggest someone you know and offer that you have a relationship with the person and would be happy to reach out. If your organization is trying to partner with a company and you have a contact there, you can say, "I'll try to get more information; I know someone over there." People will care about your network, and thus assign value to it, if it serves them. If your network can't help them at all, keep your mouth shut. Saying, "Oh I went to lunch yesterday with so-and-so, we go way back" is not valuable, it's obnoxious. You need to at least give your company, or your managers, the *perception* that one day they can call upon you and you might provide access. Whether or not it happens, it needs to be a possibility.

Putting In the Work

If you show up at a new job on day one and it already seems like everyone around you knows the right people or is involved in a number of organizations or is already on associate boards that make them look good, it can feel like you are starting from behind. You all might have the same title, but they seem to have more value. This doesn't mean you can't catch up. The best way to acquire value if you start from behind is through performance. Doing good work counts for a lot. If you are delivering work product at a high level, with a good attitude and on time, people will notice.

That said, you have to be consistent. Doing something once—even if it's something impressive—doesn't add value. It can too easily be written off as a fluke. A lot of workers think they are better than they are because they do one impressive thing. As the CEO of ColorComm, I am not wowed by one success. It's great, don't get me wrong, and I appreciate it. But if you have one win, I'm not saying, "We can't lose her! She's too valuable!" But if you establish a pattern of producing? If I can rely on the fact that you will succeed at whatever task you take on? Now you are a high performer, and that's valuable to the company and it's valuable to me as a boss.

Once you have established your value and you see it increase over time, it's important to remember that value needs to translate to . . . something. It doesn't have to translate to more money (though it should eventually!), but it should at the very least translate to a better experience in some way that is important to you. A lot of what goes into loving where you work is being at a company that meets your quality-of-life parameters—maybe your employer lets you work from home a few days a week or they make it easy for you to take appointments during the day. Maybe they approve your request to be fully remote. Maybe they foot the bill for professional development courses or send you to a high-profile industry conference or give you a seat at the company table for an annual gala. Companies can't do this for every employee, but if you have added value—meaning that you are giving something extra to the company—they should be giving you something in return.

I say all this because too often, I've seen the opposite happen. A woman acquires value by doing the work and putting in the effort, and rather than being met with flexibility or other benefits, she is only met with more work. A company knows she is a producer, so they ask more of her. *Oh, Lauren works fast and doesn't need her hand held, so let's give her more to do! Let's give her tighter deadlines since we know she can meet them.* This is not the goal! Increasing your value should not translate to a more unpleasant experience. So again, keep track of your wins. Document your good feedback. If someone writes an e-mail that says, *Amazing work, I didn't even need to make any changes*, put that in an accolades folder in your inbox. Because yes, we are fighting for equality in the workplace, but we want equality based on our work product and we don't all offer the same end result. Not all of us can deliver certain clients or bring in revenue. You should be accommodated or treated well based on meeting the needs of the company. What you bring in should dictate what they will bring to you. So think about what you need in exchange for the added value you are offering your employers so that you can ask for what you need when the time comes.

If You Don't Believe It, Why Should They?

Getting hired isn't easy. There are usually interviews to ace, managers to win over, hoops to jump through. By the time you are logging on to your company's server, someone has decided that you can do the job. But there's something much more important than your boss or co-workers believing you can do the job: YOU need to believe you can do the job. At the end of the day, knowing your value is about *believing in* your value. It's about confidence. You need to know that you bring something valuable to the table. Because if you question yourself, everyone else is going to follow suit.

For some women of color, specifically Black women, confidence is one area where we excel. Research has repeatedly shown that Black women have higher self-esteem than white or Hispanic women—Black women are more likely to use words like *successful* or *beautiful* to describe ourselves than women of other races. That confidence can feel like necessary armor in a world that is constantly questioning us or putting us down. Still, it can be hard to project that confidence if we are constantly worried about appearing *pushy* or *aggressive* or *angry* in the office.

I once hired an employee at ColorComm whom I was extremely excited about. Our whole team was. Based on her interviews and past experience, we had no question that she would be able to execute the work that was required of her. Yet the moment this employee walked through our office doors on her first day, it was clear she didn't believe in herself. Everything about her presence communicated that she felt overwhelmed and scared, and that she questioned her own ability. By day three she was saying out loud, "I don't know if I can do it." As a hiring manager, that's not what you want to hear. Think about it. When you're in a meeting about a work project, do you want the other person to say, "I *think* I can do it; at least, I hope . . . but I'm not sure"? Or would you rather hear "No problem, I've got this. You don't need to worry"? We can probably all agree that the second response inspires more confidence. Even if that person says, "I've actually never done this before. I'm confident I'll figure it out. Thanks for trusting me. I'll let you know if I run into any trouble," their confidence in their ability to get the work done will inspire your own. Believing in yourself is something of a fake-it-'til-you-make-it situation—even if you aren't sure that you can handle a project, your manager doesn't need to know that. Pretend to feel confident, and then figure it out. And to be clear, that doesn't mean you can't ask questions. Asking smart and specific questions says you aren't winging it, that you are smart enough to know what you don't know and to get the necessary information to do the job right. But if you walk around saying, "I can't do it," or acting scared, why should anyone believe you can do it? With that ColorComm employee, I could only say "Good job" so much. If you are insecure or don't believe you can do the work, I can't help you. In the end, she was so insecure, so doubtful of her own abilities, she barely made it to the three-month mark before more or less firing herself.

Beware the Devaluation

Just as it is in your power to increase your value in the workplace, it is also in your power to *devalue* yourself. A great attitude, a reputation as a team player who people actively want to work with—these things will help lift up an individual whose work product is good enough but not great. On the flip side, if you are someone whose work is good enough, but you come into the office with an air of entitlement or you're constantly asking for special treatment, your good-enough work might suddenly not be valuable enough for a company to keep you on. These negatives detract from your value.

I've seen this happen at ColorComm a number of times. It's amazing what you witness and hear when you're on the hiring end of things, and it's clear to me that employees who are devaluing themselves truly have no idea. They have no sense of how their actions or requests are perceived. I once had an employee who had so many wants, not needs—she had all these stipulations for work, all these requests, and she made them well before she'd been at the company long enough for us to know or value her work product. This was a midlevel manager who we were so excited to hire—she came in, she interviewed well, she had great experience personally and professionally. She had overcome adversity, she was smart; we thought she would be a home-run addition to the company. But the day she came in she started asking for all these accommodations. Could she leave early on Mondays and

Wednesdays? Could she come in late Tuesday and Friday? The whole company used PCs, but could she get a Mac? In isolation, a few requests are no big deal, but when they amount to a pattern of behavior, you start decreasing your own value. In this woman's first few weeks on the job, we took her across the country to L.A. for a work event. We were travelling together as a team and this new hire immediately asked to amend her itinerary so she could fly at a more convenient time for her. Now, to bring someone on a work trip when she was still so new to the company was a big deal for us. It's a big deal for any company. Please, take note: if your employer sends you out of state to represent the company at an industry event, that is a sign that they value you. They are financially investing in your career trajectory to put you in a space where they need a representative—maybe at a conference, maybe at a work event, maybe to attend an industry awards ceremony—and more important, they are choosing you to represent the company in that moment. It's a vote of confidence because usually when you travel you will be interfacing with clients or other important players. In one of my early positions in PR, I was sent to Las Vegas for the annual technology trade show CES. I was so psyched. Lots of people wanted this opportunity, and I was very cognizant of that. Those kinds of trips ask a lot of you, but if you play them right and you're on your best behavior, they can be great for your career trajectory because a ton of growth opportunities come out of these experiences. In the case of my employee, we asked her to accompany us to L.A. for an event we were hosting at the Waldorf Astoria in Beverly Hills. She immediately made clear that the hours we proposed weren't convenient for her. Could she leave later? Could she stay at a different hotel? Eventually her requests became so much that she lost value to our company. Her work product was fine, but it wasn't good enough to warrant the constant accommodating that she deemed necessary. We ended up parting ways.

That's just one story of many. The details in each case might look different, but the end result is the same. I've had employees who regularly called in "sick" on Mondays because their weekends got a little too rowdy. I had an employee who asked to work remotely for six months—this was well before the pandemic, before remote work was common—because our company had moved to New York but she had kids and she didn't want to leave in the middle of a school year. That seemed reasonable, so we approved the request—her work product was good enough that we felt she deserved it. After we granted this request, she continued to ask for exceptions for things that other employees were not receiving. Eventually we had to question why this person felt entitled to special treatment that no one else received.

Value goes both ways. As you navigate the professional space, you can increase your own value, or you can significantly decrease it. It's all in your control, but that's the importance of self-assessment. You need to constantly appraise what you bring to the table. How are your bosses responding to your work product? How is your attitude? Do your colleagues want to work with you? Be honest with yourself. It's easy to overestimate your performance—to assume that as long as you're meeting the job requirements you are doing a good job. But it's not that simple. If you're leaning into the "quiet quitting" trend, you may be able to coast for three months, maybe even a year, but be aware of how it looks to the decision-makers around you. You will not build a career with an upward trajectory if you are doing the bare minimum and nothing more. If you want to move up, you need to perform, and you need to know where you stand. And it's not just about getting kudos—having a sense of your own performance and how it is perceived will protect you from being blindsided when layoffs come. I've had to fire a number of people (and I've been fired myself), and the common theme in each of those instances was how surprised the person was. These people did not see it coming! They were all so shocked, hurt, mad at the company—almost always putting the blame on other people. But what that reaction tells me, every single time, is that this person was not checking in with themselves. They were not taking an honest look at what they were bringing to the table. Because here's a promise: if you do not consistently increase your own value—to yourself and, more important, to your organization—your company will eventually find someone else for your role who absolutely will. And if your self-assessment tells you that you *are* continually adding more and more value, then great! That's just more data to support your bid for whatever perks you think you deserve.

— 5 —

YOU NEED . . .
TO TAKE
(CALCULATED) RISKS

In 2013, when ColorComm was about 2 years old and I was 28, I was nominated for *PR Week*'s 40 Under 40 list. It's a pretty huge award in the PR industry—insiders know and respect it, and placement on the list can quickly land you "rising star" status. Professionals who make the list are usually executive vice presidents at their agencies—people who've spent years climbing the corporate ladder—and I was working at the crisis communications firm as a communications strategist. Still, I was working on the side as the founder of a company that was doing important work and starting to get some buzz. While the award seemed like a long shot, it was a shot worth taking.

For honors like this one, organizations have to submit nominations. Given my midlevel position, I knew the firm would never nominate me—at least not yet—so I was happy ColorComm submitted the awards entry. I wanted ColorComm to be recognized for our work, and I knew that making the list could mean big things for my career and the company I was building. What I didn't spend time worrying about was the protocol or the politics of it all—how the firm would feel about my nomination. If I won, would it rub people the wrong way? I thought I was deserving of the award, so I was happy to have my name submitted. If it made people mad, I could always ask for forgiveness later.

You can probably guess how this story ends. Not only did I get the award, but I was the youngest person to receive the honor that year. But there was one "problem" (in quotes because, frankly, it wasn't a problem for me): only one person from any given company can be named to the list in a year. My nomination was submitted by ColorComm, but when I won, it was on behalf of the firm and ColorComm—the article touted both my day job and the organization I was building while I was off the clock. I didn't give much thought to this stipulation when I agreed to have my name put forward. I was just going after what I wanted. But after I won? Not everybody was thrilled. In fact, one day while I was working in the New York office—I'd traveled to Manhattan from Washington, D.C., where I was living at the time —a white male senior vice president began schooling me on the award. Did I know what a big deal it was? Did I know that I'd taken someone else's spot at the company? It turned out that this guy was nominated by the firm and he had been expecting to win. He seemed to think he was a shoo-in until I swooped in and "stole" what he thought was his. I know now that this is not necessarily an unusual experience for women of color, but when this man confronted me, I was caught completely off-guard. My mouth just dropped. It was incredibly uncomfortable, and, sure, if we'd been measured on corporate titles alone, he would have been the clear winner. But I'd been putting in hours of work on the side to build a company that was changing our industry for the better. And who's to say that if I hadn't won, this guy would have? Tons of names are submitted each year, so there's a perfectly good chance that no one from our firm would have even made the list if I hadn't. But that didn't matter to him. My colleague clearly felt that I did not belong in this prestigious space. He felt entitled to something that I got instead, and he was pissed. And the truth is, plenty of communications strategists might have sat back and "waited their turn" for the nomination, but I'd already learned the pitfalls of waiting for success to come to you. I took a risk and went after what I wanted.

I still remember the day I got the call from the firm's head of global communications telling me that I made the list. He admitted that his first reaction, when the magazine told him that I'd earned the honor, was "Who is Lauren Wesley Wilson?" That became a running joke—*Lauren Wesley Wilson? Who's she?*—because until that moment, I'd been relatively unknown at the company. I was doing good work and making relationships and proving my value to my immediate bosses, but this was a big organization and I was many levels from the top. The C-Suite was not aware of me . . . yet. But that changed overnight. Now that I was a noted "up-and-comer," I suddenly brought even more value to the organization. (Sometimes it takes an outside organization recognizing your value for your own company to catch up. It's like in every romantic comedy ever, when the guy doesn't know how good he has it until someone else wants his girlfriend.) The CEO of the firm called me directly to congratulate me, and she bought a table at the 40 Under 40 celebration event so that senior leaders at the organization could show their support. I got a promotion. Recruiters started calling because everyone wants to poach the rising stars. I was in demand in a brand-new way—a way I'd been working toward for my entire career—all because I'd put my name out there, taken a risk, and won an award that I didn't ask permission to go after.

Redefining Risk

Risk-taking is a critical aspect of career-building. It's a must if you want to establish yourself as a major player in your field. Playing it safe doesn't inspire anyone to stop and take notice. It might make you reliable and dependable, and there is value in that, but it will rarely help you advance. The way I see it, risks are simply actions that are not in your comfort zone. They're opportunities that may not be explicitly outlined in the company handbook, but that doesn't mean they're bad or wrong. It simply means that their outcomes are uncertain. Of course, if the outcome of every professional decision were clear, we'd all take the same path. The truth is, taking a risk—and by *risk* I mean making a calculated, thought-out decision to try something new or different, I'm not talking about throwing caution to the wind and doing something stupid on a whim—is about taking the pieces of yourself you value most and asking, *How can I grow this a little more, in a new way?* That might mean, as it did for me, going after an award so you are recognized in a specific industry and thus get more opportunity. It might mean pursuing a promotion or investing your own money into getting an additional degree or certification. It might be creating a social media account that showcases your skills. In the moment when you do any of those things, they feel risky because there is no guarantee that they will work out. Still, taking a risk is about creating an accelerated path to a desired outcome. And much of the time, the same actions that many women characterize as "risky," men consider run-of-the-mill. Consider these results from Big Four accounting firm and professional services network KPMG's 2019 Women's Leadership Study titled "Risk, Resilience, Reward," which found that only 43 percent of women say they are "open to taking the bigger risks associated with career advancement."[1] (And women only get more hesitant the longer they are in the workplace: when it comes to women with more than 15 years of work experience, only 37 percent say they are open to taking big risks, compared to 45 percent of women with less than 5 years of experience.) According to the study, the "risks" women are most hesitant to take include promoting their own accomplishments, volunteering for a big presentation, asking for a higher salary, and moving for a job. As far as I can tell, the actions on that list aren't even true risks! I would describe them as required parts of being a professional. Self-promotion? Volunteering for work? How on earth would a person get ahead without doing these things? I can promise you that a man would not consider any of these things risks.

For women of color, these actions are especially critical. Take asking for a higher salary. Research shows very clearly that women of color are not being handed salary bumps at the same rate as others—according to research from LeanIn.Org, for every 100 white men promoted, only 68 Latinas and 58 Black women are promoted.[2] If we sit back and wait for advancement opportunities to be handed to us, we could be waiting a long time. (I will note that this same study found that "women of color are the biggest potential risk-takers, with 57 percent saying they are open to taking big risks to further their careers versus 38 percent of white women."[3] Makes sense, since we're the least likely to get ahead without them.)

I get why it can be scary to make the so-called "risky" moves, especially for those of us who were taught our whole lives to keep our heads down, try to fit in, and not make waves. Raising your hand to lead a project or make a presentation, putting yourself up for awards—these actions all shine a greater spotlight on you, and that means people will be watching if things don't work out. Your boss might say no when you ask for a raise (research shows that "Black job seekers are expected to negotiate less than their White counterparts and are penalized in negotiations with lower salary outcomes"—in other words, if you're Black, you're likely to get a smaller raise when you ask for one than your white counterparts) or you may be told you're not ready for a higher title, both of which can make you feel foolish or unappreciated.[4] You may not win the award you put yourself up for, or your presentation may be a flop—this can be embarrassing, especially when your colleagues are paying attention. I won't sugarcoat that because part of taking chances is understanding the consequences if things don't go your way. And the fallout from these risks can feel even more significant as a woman of color because there is often this sense that we are representing not just ourselves but our entire race or gender. If your white colleague's presentation is a flop, it is a commentary on that specific colleague. When a woman of color botches the same opportunity, there will be individuals who will extrapolate that error—it's not about *your* ability to present, but that of Black women or Hispanic women or brown women in general. Research shows that women of color, and Black women especially, feel on guard or closely watched in their work because their actions or performance will reflect on others who look like them.[5] But when it comes to your career, taking risks is really about reframing your thinking. So much of what women of color are taught about professionalism is about waiting . . . Wait for review time, wait for the next pay cycle, wait for someone to invite you to join this committee or that professional network. At one of my early jobs, there was an executive, Nancy, who was a clear power player within the company. I knew that getting in with Nancy could help my career because people took her input or recommendations seriously. One day, I mentioned to one of my colleagues that I was going to ask Nancy to coffee. "You don't ask Nancy to coffee," my co-worker said. "Nancy asks you." I remember how much that scared me. *Wow*, I thought. *I've got to wait for her to notice me? How will she ever get to know who I am if I'm just sitting around waiting? That hasn't worked for me in the past!* Still, I was intimidated—so much so that I never did ask Nancy to coffee. I didn't even ask her for a 15-minute phone call. They say the risks you regret most are the ones you didn't take, and I have to say, I've asked a lot of people to coffee in my career, and this is the only invitation (or lack thereof) that I still remember. What I know now is that the rules of who you can speak to or what accolades you can go after are not rules you need to live by.

There's another reason, of course, why the waiting game won't serve your career. The truth is, not everyone at your company will have your best interests at heart, and not everyone will want you to get ahead. This could be for any number of reasons—they may see you as competition, they may mentor someone at your level who they want to help excel, they may simply not like you. Who knows their motivations, and frankly, who cares? You can't control how other people feel about you, only how you behave. You simply need to know that nobody is thinking about your career the way you're thinking about it, which is why you need to decide if a risk is worth taking. I often talk to ColorComm members who are frustrated that their bosses don't care about their goals, and I always say the same thing: everyone is focused on themselves. It may sound cynical, but I don't mean it as a bad thing. That's the way it should be! Everyone should be working on their own advancement. In fact, I find it empowering to know that you alone are in control of your career because it means you have every right—and responsibility—to go after what you want. Build relationships, attend industry functions, pursue awards. If you want to oversee specific areas of the business and understand the P&L, jump right in and offer to take on the spreadsheets. If you want a better understanding of your niche industry, volunteer for an associate board so you can make connections—and then make sure to tell your boss about it. You can't increase your own value without communicating that you've done the extra work. I liken it to going to school. Back in college, you probably didn't just go to class. You had to study, do extra credit, raise your hand, join study groups. Jobs are no different— every risk you take is a decision to go after your success.

Every risk you take in the workplace should be calculated. You should always think through possible outcomes and consequences, and you should always have a plan. Sure, inherent in taking a risk is the chance that things won't work out as you hoped, but if you have clear goals and a well-constructed vision for your career, then your actions, even the risky ones—especially the risky ones!— will usually align with that plan. You will be able to articulate a clear reason why you took the risk (especially important for those times when said risk backfires). You should take these chances not just to see what might happen, but because the desired outcome will move you along your planned path more quickly. You are nothing, after all, if not a savvy businesswoman.

Working the Side Hustle

These days, one of the most common risks I see women taking—and I used to be one of these women—is pursuing a side hustle. To be clear, I'm not talking about a hobby or an extracurricular. Being a marathon runner is not a side hustle. Nor is pursuing a master's degree at night. I'm talking about a profit-seeking business, or a not-for-profit that still runs like a business—something that *could* one day be a full-time job but is, at least currently, a side gig to your *actual* full-time job. According to the 2019 annual "State of Women-Owned Businesses Report," a survey commissioned by American Express, women of color are starting businesses at a higher rate than any other demographic.[6] "Minority women are more likely to have a side hustle," wrote *Fast Company* about the report. "Over the last five years, the number of women with side hustles has increased to 39 percent, compared to a 21 percent average rate of entrepreneurship. Among minority women, it's even higher: 65 percent compared to 32 percent, respectively." For women of color who feel stifled by the inequitable conditions of Corporate America, a side hustle can feel like a way out and a clear path toward independence. Still, any work you do on the side—especially work that demands a lot of your time and attention—is a risk. There are a lot of unknown variables that could end up working against you. For example, you're taking a chance that, at least until that side hustle becomes your full-time hustle, it won't negatively affect your work performance. You're making an assumption that your higher-ups or co-workers won't mind that your attention is divided. You're taking a risk that you aren't somehow competing with your day job in a way that could get you into trouble, and that your employer won't mind being associated with whatever side gig you're working on, because you, as their employee, ultimately represent them.

I am all for the side hustle. We should all be getting paid to pursue our passions. But it needs to be pursued with caution. As long as you are employed by a company that is paying you a salary and benefits, that company needs to be your top priority . . . or, at least, the people at that company need to *feel* like they're your top priority. I once had a junior employee who did pretty decent work—she wasn't an absolute superstar, but she certainly wasn't bad. She worked for ColorComm for two years, but one of the factors that kept getting in the way of her success was her second job. She would often leave 15 or 20 minutes early to make it on time to her side gig. Not a huge deal once or twice, but when this became a pattern of behavior, of course we began to question her commitment. At some point, we had a big work event in New York to launch a media platform and, because of her side hustle, this employee was unable to go when we needed all hands on deck. She didn't prioritize the company's big moment, and still she was very taken aback and confused and upset when she was fired as a result. So my advice? Unless it is explicitly stated in your company handbook that you need to disclose any side gigs you're working on, keep it to yourself. Don't give anyone any reason to question your dedication to your job or your work ethic. Don't jeopardize your day job unless you feel very confident that you don't need it.

Now, for career women who are hoping to one day turn their side gig into their full-time focus, the most important factor in ensuring the risk works in your favor is good planning. (This could be said for so much of career building— knowing your goals and coming up with specific plans to achieve them is the key to most success.) Start by figuring out how much savings you'll need before you can leave your current job to pursue the side hustle full-time—it should be the equivalent of three to six months' salary, if not more. Once you've narrowed in on a number, you need to establish a clear blueprint for how you're going to get there. It will probably entail foregoing vacations and fancy restaurant dinners for a bit. Consider yourself warned. Then, think about your schedule. When will you have time to dedicate to your side work while you're still fully employed elsewhere? Because you shouldn't be using your official workday, or your official work devices, for anything other than work for the company that currently pays your salary. You very well might have signed a contract saying you won't use company property for outside work, but you also don't want to give your job any support for a claim that you are not committed to and focused on the work at hand. Any attention and energy given to your side hustle should, in fact, be on the side.

Back when I started ColorComm, I was living in a small D.C. apartment with slow dial-up Internet, so I spent two hours before work and two hours after work using the free Wi-Fi at the Marriott hotel across the street. It was a lot—long days, too little sleep, morning workouts and evening drinks missed in favor of doing more work—but it was worth it to me because I knew my dream was to one day leave my firm and run ColorComm full-time. I was willing to put in the extra hours. But if reading this makes you cringe with dread, or if you just don't want to spend that much time working, that's okay! It is not necessary to work from dawn to dusk every single day in order to have a successful career. But that reaction also means you probably shouldn't plan to make your side hustle your full-time job anytime soon, because you may not be passionate enough or hungry enough to make it happen. For some people, the idea of dedicating hours upon hours to a side gig is invigorating. The notion of building something of your own and being the one in charge gives you a buzz. If you're wondering if this risk is for you, that buzz is what you are looking for. That's what will keep you going, down the road, when business is slow or clients leave.

When I finally worked up the courage—and the savings—to leave my comfortable corporate job to run ColorComm full-time, it was not easy. People in my life thought I was crazy. This was before entrepreneurship was constantly showcased on social media, so there were fewer public examples of what I was trying to do. I was taking a major gamble, risking my steady paycheck and paid vacation days for a chance to run my own company and build something impactful . . . all at 29 years old. But at this point, ColorComm, the business, was growing. It wasn't sustainable anymore with me employed somewhere else because it had become full-time work. I couldn't make the company any bigger without giving it more of my time, and there simply weren't any more hours in the morning or at night. It needed my 8-hour (or, who are we kidding, 10-hour) business day. So I spent an entire summer considering my options and formulating a plan. I made sure I had the budget to hire an employee from the get-go so the entire company didn't fall to me. I wrote business plans for our first three months, six months, and full year. I tried to leave as little to chance as possible, but still, you don't know what you don't know, and even though I was prepared, I was scared. I was making a big bet on myself, and that's a risk no matter how much prep work you do.

When my new career got underway, it wasn't easy. In many ways, I was in over my head. My first big project was hosting the ColorComm Conference in Miami—a three-day conference at the Ritz-Carlton that took a year to plan.

I was recruiting sponsorships, managing panels, and bringing together hundreds of women of color from across the country, most of whom were more senior and more experienced than I was. I had to convince them that coming to my conference would be worth their time and valuable for their careers. And while that was exciting and fulfilling, it could also be challenging and slow-going and humbling, and, absolutely, there were days when I wanted to quit. In retrospect, I wouldn't trade any of it, but there were growing pains, lots of them, and the thing that kept my eyes on the prize was my passion for the mission and the work. I wanted to change the communications industry, to make a difference, and the excitement about that prospect ultimately won out.

This is why I say you need to have the passion if you're going to take the risk. Because when there are hard times—and there will be hard times—and you're scared and worried and wondering if you should have taken such a risky leap, you'll stick it out as long as you're doing something that fuels you. Entrepreneurship is glorified constantly—who doesn't want to go on vacation whenever she wants and get her nails done during the workday and make her own schedule? But I promise you, 90 percent of the entrepreneurship life is not glamorous, it's repetitive and grueling and maybe a little bit boring—not the kind of thing that makes for good social content. If you're gonna do it, you have to really want it.

Building Your Personal Brand

Of course, not everyone is interested in a side hustle. Yet even for those who are happy in their career but want to climb the ladder and land in the C-Suite, there's still extracurricular work to be done. As we already know, doing good work is required, but it's not enough. These days, there's an ever-increasing emphasis on building your personal brand. The rise of the corporate celebrity is a relatively new concept, but it's one that, if worked to your advantage, can increase your value within your company while also raising your profile throughout your industry. And the higher your profile, the easier it will be for future employers to see what you can do, who you know, and how you get results. Look at Bozoma Saint John, former chief marketing officer of Netflix, or Eva Chen, vice president of fashion at Meta. These women put in years of hard work and rose to the very top of their fields (don't let anyone say they were overnight sensations), but they built their personal brands along the way. They became known independently of the companies they worked for, which is part of how they became increasingly in demand and high profile as they moved from one company to the next. In both cases, the women started by building networks within their chosen fields—making connections and spearheading business partnerships or public campaigns in tech and fashion, respectively—and as their stars rose within their industries, their reputations began to grow more widely. Over time, they weren't known just in their fields, but across the business landscape, and eventually, in the social media and public landscapes, too. I bet a lot of people who know who Eva Chen is couldn't necessarily tell you where she works. They know her for her personal brand—her Insta content and her Fashion Week appearances and her #evachenpose. So how did Eva and Bozoma do it? Well, to start, neither woman has ever been shy about publicizing who they connect or partner with. They embrace opportunities to speak on panels or deliver keynotes, and they use their titles and company names to fuel both their own interests and the interests of their companies. And they are good at what they do, which means they reflect well on their companies. If you use your name and company affiliation to get the spotlight, and then you can actually deliver—meaning your public work furthers the interests of both you and your company—everybody wins.

Now, to be clear, these women are extreme cases. Bozoma Saint John has hosted a podcast with Katie Couric. Eva Chen has 2 million–plus Instagram followers and is a mainstay at the Met Gala. Your goal should not necessarily be to replicate their careers, but to recognize the value-add when you become known as an influential player or a go-to source on whatever your specialty might be. The nice thing about today's world of influencing and social media is that you don't have to wait for anyone else to promote your experience. If you want to be a high-profile player in the diversity-and-inclusion space, if you want to be the go-to source for all things brand marketing, if you want to be the one who makes financial planning accessible, you can make that happen. And this kind of personal-brand building is especially important for women of color, because, again, it's one of the few things you can control. You can't help it if nepotism didn't work in your favor, or if you didn't come into your job through connections, or if your background is different from the backgrounds of all the employees around you. But you can decide to pursue a specialty and publicize that.

In order to build your personal brand, start by asking yourself: What do you want to be known for? This question is key. And the answer shouldn't be something general like "I want to be known for my work" or "I want to be known for being smart." Get specific. You want to be known for making complicated legal topics digestible for Gen Z. You want to be known for spotlighting books written by women of color. You want to be known for being a woman in the male-dominated investment space. Once you are clear on that goal, start making concrete offerings in your professional space, because your personal brand needs to be tied to something specific. Get out there and speak on this topic, write about it, talk about it in those networking calls with people more senior than you. Being an avid Instagrammer or networking junkie is not, in itself, a brand. Visibility for visibility's sake doesn't add value. If you are on social media but not doing any actual work . . . your personal brand will have no staying power. So do your research and then volunteer to speak on panels, apply for conferences, attend networking events. When appropriate, get yourself nominated for awards or apply to be on judging committees. And yes, social media is a part of this equation—posting compelling content in your chosen space will help you establish yourself—but the tweets and stories should be a *complement* to what you do; they aren't the main event, and they certainly aren't the starting point. There are plenty of people who are extremely well-known in my industry who don't even have social media accounts. Philip Thomas, chairman of Cannes Lions, is barely on Instagram, but the man brings more than 65,000 people together every year for the Cannes Lions International Festival of Creativity—the work speaks for itself, and everyone in the business knows who he is. On the other hand, I've seen folks on Instagram who have a ton of followers but then the actual players in their fields don't even know who they are. They're so busy posting online that they forget to put in the face time in real life. They choose retweeting over actual meetings, when the reality is you will never get ahead if other people can't vouch for you. You have to build your reputation the old-fashioned way. Remember, Instagram is the vehicle for *awareness* of the work, it's not the work itself. If you want to truly build your brand, you have to do the work, because that's how you elevate your reputation.

So, what's so risky about personal-brand building? Everything I've said so far probably sounds like a surefire win. And it is, if it goes well. But, as we already know, every bit of added attention also adds risk. A notable personal brand might get the attention of the C-Suite, but it also comes with more exposure. You might make an off-the-cuff comment on a panel that doesn't land well and reflects poorly on your company. Suddenly you're wishing the C-Suite didn't notice you after all. Colleagues may feel you're distracted, worried more about your own image than the work product. You might get a fact wrong in a speech and look like you don't know what you're talking about or like you're making stuff up to get ahead. And we all know that social media comes with its own set of risks. What you post on the Internet lives forever, and cancel culture is real. Your fall can happen twice as quickly as your rise, so make sure you don't post anything that could be deemed inappropriate by your company, that goes against your company's ethos, or that showcases personal work on company time. There are also real risks attached to public speaking. Yes, it will raise your profile, but it's important to be clear from the outset about whether you're speaking on your own behalf or your company's—and if you are getting paid for any sort of public event, make sure that's permitted by your organization. If you're going to be a risk-taker you need to have all your ducks in a row and you need to have done your research. Don't leave anything up to chance that you don't have to. Getting paid for outside speaking events, for example, might be forbidden by your company, and believe me, you don't want to find out about that the hard way. There will be times when the rules of the company will have to take priority over your own personal ambitions. That's where the necessity of having a plan comes into play—not just so that you don't get into trouble, but so that you can make an informed decision about whether a risk is worth it.

You Can't Be a People Pleaser

Clearly, I believe in making the big bets and taking chances. They almost always pay off. Even if the immediate outcome is a bust, you usually learn something valuable that will ultimately serve your career. Maybe you'll discover what not to do, or how to manage a crisis, or how to persevere after a failure. It's all valuable intel. Still, it's important to keep in mind that with every new chance you take, there's an increased possibility of pissing someone off. Ruffling feathers comes with the territory. If you raise your hand to run a new project or team and it doesn't go well, other people will be negatively affected. Hopefully you've earned enough goodwill that one failed risk won't hurt too much, but it's something to keep in mind. When I won 40 Under 40, I know I made at least one person mad. Obviously, though, I have no regrets. That acknowledgement helped fast-track my career, and the guy who didn't get it? He's doing just fine, I'm sure. There will always be people who believe they're deserving of a specific career or accolade, and they will resent anything or anyone who gets in their way—even if they did far less work for it than the person who beat them out. The world will always be full of entitled individuals. We will never get ahead by focusing on pleasing others at the expense of promoting ourselves. That doesn't mean you should shove people aside or treat anyone poorly in pursuit of your own ambitions, but you can't sacrifice your success because someone else might be disappointed. And the truth is, more often than not, I find that people are only truly bothered by a person's "corporate celebrity" if that person doesn't have the work product to back it up. If someone gets attention that is rightfully earned, colleagues may roll their eyes or feel jealous, but they won't be able to log any real complaints because the productivity will be there. And usually, when a hard-working employee gets recognition they deserve, people will applaud it.

But when someone spends their time on their personal brand at the expense of doing good work? That's when things get dicey. I recently hired an employee whose personal brand was very strong, and I was thrilled to add her to our roster, but it turned out she wasn't any good at her actual job. She was great at calling attention to her work, but not so much at executing it. I found it incredibly annoying, because this was someone who was building out her professional profile on my company's time. If you're getting coveted invites or other perks as an employee of my company, I expect that you'll use that access to talk about the company and promote the good work we do—this is what any employer will expect. If you're getting media coverage and landing invitations to do amazing things, the companies that employ you—and thus are paying for your travel or letting you off work so you can go do those amazing things—are going to expect amazing performance in return. So make sure that you can live up to your platform, or it might all come crashing down.

And one final note for all the would-be risk-takers out there: start now. Young employees, especially young women of color, often think they need to wait to take the big risks—wait until they have more years under their belt, or more accolades to tout, or more connections to capitalize on. They are waiting to build up the nerve and the credibility. I understand this inclination, but the truth is that taking risks only gets harder as you progress in your career because you have more to lose and further to fall. Remember that statistic from the beginning of this chapter? Women are significantly less inclined to take professional risks as they get more workplace experience under their belt. As you get older, you need to be even more calculating—maybe you have a family or a partner you need to factor into your career decision, maybe you've built a reputation and there is more visibility if you take a chance that doesn't pay off. I've had plenty of failures in my career, and even I get nervous when it's time to pursue the next big thing because I've got more eyes on me now. I'm not saying it's not worth it, but there will always be a reason to avoid taking the next big leap. It will always be scary, and as you ascend the corporate ladder, the stakes will only get higher. So, start today. Make the scary choice, because one thing I can assure you of? No one ever got noticed by playing it safe.

— 6 —

YOU NEED . . .
TO DO THE WORK

Every single trick of the trade included in this book—the relationship-building, the risk-taking, the self-promoting—assumes that you are already doing good work. That's the baseline. If you aren't consistently executing your work at a high level, the rest of it doesn't matter. And this is especially true for women of color, who are often the first on the chopping block when companies make cuts—last hired, first fired, as the expression goes. What your specific work looks like will vary between industries, but good work usually boils down to the same factors, whether it's the little things, like meeting deadlines, or the bigger things, like bringing in revenue, managing budgets, and driving strategic decisions.

When I see employees doing mediocre work, it's not always because they are phoning it in or half-assing the job. Sometimes that *is* what's happening—especially in this new "work from anywhere" climate where people are taking calls from vacation or executing deals from their iPhone. Work ethic has absolutely changed post-pandemic. People just don't want to dedicate the same amount of effort they once did, which should work in favor of those of us who take our careers seriously and are willing to put in the work. But sometimes, the people I see doing just-okay work are doing so because no one ever taught them differently. They don't know what they don't know. So I want to take a moment in this chapter to go over the fundamentals. If no one ever told you what good work looks like, I'm telling you now.

Back to Basics

If you're reading this book, you probably think you already know the basics of good work—arrive on time, meet deadlines, check your work, treat your colleagues with respect. These sound like simple guidelines, yet they are surprisingly hard for many of us to follow consistently. When we get caught up in the grind, we forget how important these basics are to how we're perceived in the workplace. Humans often grapple with negativity bias— we give more weight to bad attributes than good ones when we're judging people—which means messing up in one area could potentially cause all our good work elsewhere to be discounted (that horns effect again). Too often we make excuses for ourselves, thinking that if we excel in one area, we can slack in another. Our weekly reports are killing it, so we can come in late. We're bringing in clients, so we can miss deadlines. But those excuses often don't fly because it's the slacking that will stand out.

Women of color are judged to a higher standard—I wish it weren't true, and part of why it's so important to get more of us in leadership positions is to change this reality. But conversations about advancing workers of color have existed for so long that, at the end of the day, if it's what people wanted, it would already have happened. I don't care how many companies pledge to uplift their colleagues of color—so far, the actions haven't backed up the words. And that makes good work doubly important—we can't provide leaders with any reason to not follow through on their promises.

Timing

Showing up to work on time, I hope, is a no-brainer. Not only on your first day, but every day. If a meeting starts at 10 A.M., be at work at 9 A.M. And when you sit down at your desk, you should already know your plan for that day. There's a real "wing it" mentality in today's work culture, so people who are prepared stand out. When you settle in on Monday morning, have you planned in advance what you need to do that day? Did you take care of yourself on your off days so you are ready for your on days? The answers should always be yes.

And just because you need to arrive on time doesn't mean you should plan to leave on time. Remember, this is a career, not just a job, and certainly not shift work where you clock in and clock out. If you are paid hourly, by all means, leave when your shift is over or bill for any overtime. But if we're talking about long-term careers and salaried professions, they are not clock-in, clock-out gigs. Sometimes you will come early and stay late. Sure, there will be times when you leave early, but if your workday ends at 6 and you are consistently closing your computer at 5:59 P.M., people will notice. It's increasingly common these days to be rigid about shutting down. A lot of Gen Zers walk out the door the minute the clock strikes 6. At my office, I've seen Gen Zers start packing up at 5:45

P.M. every day. And these are people on salary. If I need to touch base with them at 6:05 P.M. or 6:10 P.M., I expect there to be some flexibility.

I'm not saying you should be held hostage by your work, sitting at your desk with nothing to do just so your boss notices that you're the last person there. And I certainly don't think it's okay for your workplace to run you ragged all hours of the day, calling you first thing in the morning or late at night or repeatedly bothering you when you're taking paid time off. But these days, employees are so worried that those things *might* happen that the first thing they do is establish their boundaries. News flash: you don't need to ask for boundaries if you are not overworked. It's time to reframe your thinking. Remember that work is a two-way street. Even in an employees' market, you should be in a reciprocal relationship with your employer; you don't need to default to "these are my needs" if no one is encroaching on them.

Remember, the fact that salaries are not hourly works in your favor. If yours was an hourly job, your boss would be clocking all your breaks, all the time you take for lunch, every time you legitimately need to leave early for a doctor's appointment or family affair. All that time you are not working would mean docked pay, and there is a lot of time in an eight-hour day when we are not working. Salaried jobs come with a level of trust and expectation—your manager trusts and expects that you will get your work done. If you need to take a break, your pay doesn't suffer, and if you need to stay late, your pay doesn't increase. Suggested hours are give and take, whether you work from home or from an office.

Deadlines

Deadlines exist for a reason. In fact, for many different reasons. It might be because your boss's boss asked for something at a certain time, or because a client has a launch on a specific date, or because work needs to be done by the end of the quarter, or because a project is tied to something in the news. I've also seen instances when deadlines are simply a test—your boss wants to know if you can get things in on time, or if you can prioritize and think strategically. The truth is, if you are given a deadline, the reason behind it doesn't matter. What you need to know is that if something is due at noon and you hand it in at 12:05 P.M., you haven't met the deadline. You are late. Generally, I take the approach of getting things in early, but not too early. You shouldn't push it to 11:59 A.M., but if you hand something in a week before it's due, it might look like you didn't give it the time and attention it required.

Of course, how quickly you should turn something around is on a fairly case-by-case basis. You may be assigned a number of projects with the same deadline, so it will be on you to figure out what needs to take priority, what can be turned around immediately, and what should take extra time. The ability to prioritize indicates an understanding of your organization's goals—it shows that you know which projects have higher stakes and can execute accordingly.

Over time, you may start to realize that no matter your deadline, your boss doesn't get around to looking at something until a few days after you've sent it in. It will be tempting to assume you can push your own due date as a result. I know this because I've tried it. I've faced down a tight deadline and thought to myself, *I know my boss doesn't need this right away, so I don't want to kill myself to get her something she won't look at until next week.* I've also been on the other end of this, dealing with an employee who delivered something late because, as she said, "I didn't think you really needed it that quickly," or "Last time you took a long time to get back to me." I told her what my boss told me back when I made the same assumptions: that is not your call. You never know when a window will open up for someone to review your work, and you want it to be on their desk, as expected, when it does.

Quality of Work

If you are delivering work to your boss or a client or a partner, I'll assume you believe it's of high quality. If you are someone who knowingly does work that's just average because you assume others will catch edits or mistakes, and you don't particularly care and just want it off your plate to get home and watch Netflix, this book probably isn't for you.

If you believe you are submitting good work, I'm not exactly equipped to tell you otherwise. I can't speak to what high-quality work looks like in your particular field, because my high-quality public relations work is going to look very different from another person's high-quality finance work, which will look different from another person's HR work or sales work or IT work. But there are ways to know if your work is where it needs to be. First, review everything you do before you hand it in. I cannot tell you how often I receive work with misspellings or careless errors because someone rushed to hand it in. Most of the time these mistakes could have been easily fixed with a once-over before hitting *send* or *submit*. Don't forgo this step because you know you'll need to revise the work anyway. Whatever you hand in should, in your estimation, be as good as final. Which leads me to my second, and even more important, point: pay attention to feedback. There is no better way to understand if your work is what it needs to be than to take note of how your work is being received. Are people saying, "Great job, this is exactly what I needed?" Are they spending a lot of time revising your work? Are you getting light edits and being trusted to make the improvements, or is there so much red pen that your boss says, "Don't worry, I'll just handle it myself." If the latter, then your work needs improvement. And that's okay; no one gets everything exactly right from the jump. But if your work needs, well, work, then you may need to ask for help. Be clear about your desire to improve.

Additionally, you want to always have a steady flow of projects. I know it's tempting to lay low when you don't have a lot on your plate so that you can have a few quiet days, but if your workload is light for an extended period of time, people will notice. They may not say anything, but that doesn't mean they don't know, so you need to raise your hand when things are slow. Show that you are pro-active. Having a continuous stretch of light workdays can be an argument to phase you out. Suddenly it's "We don't have a need for you; we don't have enough work." Your lack of assignments could be used as a data point to show why you shouldn't get a promotion or more money—"Oh sorry, you aren't maximizing your workflow." You may not want to be at capacity, but you'll feel different if and when lay-offs come.

Reading the Room: Communication, Dress Code, Administrative Tasks

Different workplaces have different communication styles. In general, you want to err on the side of being more formal. Don't use emojis or a million exclamation points in your e-mails. Don't use flowery fonts or colors. These things reek of nonprofessionalism or not taking your job seriously.

Soon after you begin at any workplace, make sure you understand the different communication platforms and how they are used. Slack and text and e-mail are not the same, and they are not used for the same things. At most companies, e-mail is more formal than Slack, and Slack is more formal than text. I once texted my boss to tell her I was running late for work, and she responded by saying, "Do not text me, this should be in an e-mail." Lesson learned. If you want to talk business, e-mail it is—it's a paper trail and can be acknowledged by HR, for better or worse. But again, these preferences are usually specific to the individual workplace, which is why being able to read the room and adapt to the workplace culture is so important.

Dress code is similar. Now, I'm not saying you need to wear what everyone else is wearing or change your personal style. I love fashion, I have my own style, and I'm not trying to look like someone else. But if I work in an office that is clearly buttoned up, I'm not going to show up in jeans. And if I work somewhere that is obviously casual, I'm not going to wear designers head to toe. It's important to understand your environment, and adjusting to the general culture—communication, wardrobe, all of it—helps communicate that understanding.

Finally, let's talk about admin work. I've been in jobs where I've been asked to be the note-taker or to get the coffee much more than my colleagues, and there was clearly a race component at play. (Research shows that women of color are more likely to be assigned or asked to take on "office housework" tasks, like taking notes, booking conference rooms, or ordering lunch.) But it's also the case that in my industry, which involves a lot of event planning and arranging interviews and similar tasks, as well as in many other industries, there is plenty of unsexy behind-the-scenes administrative work. Scheduling meetings, making sure travel logistics are handled . . . it's not glamorous, and it can be tempting to offload these tasks to assistants. Sometimes that's okay, but again, you need to read the room. If the vibe at your company is that all hands are on deck, you cannot be too good for the unglamorous stuff. This is one area where being a team player comes in—doing this work well, and with a smile, will pay off. It will help you understand the infrastructure of the organization and what it takes to run the business. It will help you understand the lay of the land before you start showing off everything you know. Like I said, it all starts with the basics.

Understanding Budgets

As you rise up in the ranks in your profession, more responsibilities will be added to your workload. In the early days, you might be just a soldier, taking commands and doing what you're told. But as you begin to prove that you're a good performer who is knowledgeable about and connected in your industry, and you show that you can lead teams or projects, you will start to move up in the ranks. Promotions into managerial positions, while exciting, can also be daunting. Your job description will probably include overseeing employees and managing a budget, which may be entirely new to you and especially tricky if you work in a field that's not generally focused on numbers. My training was in public relations—writing press releases, placing media interviews, scheduling book tours—so it was a big change when I was suddenly asked to project a budget or operationalize spending. And this is true in nearly every field. Budgeting is the kind of task that workers often have to learn on the fly.

By the time you get into a role where you need to develop a budget, you likely know more than you think. You probably know what roles are necessary on your team. You should have access to the department's existing budget, so you can see how money has been allocated in the past. You probably have a sense of what expenses are nonnegotiable and what are nice-to-haves, as well as how much revenue different projects bring in. What you don't know, ask! Before you get too deep into any sort of line-item work, you should have a sense from the C-Suite of what your team or department's overall budget projections will be; can you expect an increase in your budget now that you've assumed the role? Are there any budget cuts on the horizon that you need to be aware of? Talk to the folks on your team, too. You may be the manager, but employees who have been in their positions for a while can help you understand individual expenses that are directly related to their work. If you oversee a marketing department, you may need to go to your art director to understand the usual costs of event photography in a given year. Ask these questions early; don't wait until time has passed and you realize you're overwhelmed or, worse, you've already made major mistakes. Screwing with the company's bottom line is not a good look.

If you're really intimidated by the numbers, you can always take a course or go to an event focused on building your budget management skills. They'll not only help you in the immediate term, but also add skills to your arsenal that will increase your value down the line. Even if your company won't foot the bill for the course, it's a worthwhile investment in yourself and your professional development.

Being trusted with a departmental budget will also give you a sense of your team's value to the organization overall. The distribution of budgets is probably the single most telling indicator of a company's priorities. The money flows to the areas that the company deems most important. "Put your money where your mouth is" is an expression for a reason. If a company talks a big game about caring about something—DEI, for example—but barely allocates any funds to getting the work done . . . well, you have your answer.

At ColorComm, we work with a lot of brands that need help understanding how to achieve their DEI goals. We recently worked with one company that needed to make changes after getting itself in hot water internally. We presented its executives with a multipronged plan, with concrete actions that would help them make strides toward the equity goals they'd publicized to their employees. The problem was that they made these promises, then got tight on budget. Their response was to cite budget constraints and claim they'd have to pick only one prong. They could do unconscious bias training, but not any of the other proposed actions, they said. The money just wasn't there. It was disappointing. With DEI especially, companies often want more for less—they want to see improvement, but they don't want to put money behind the problem. That's not how operations function. If you have a lean budget, you are probably going to get lean results. Part of the problem is that DEI as a top-level priority is new to so many companies that they don't even know what the department budget should be. Organizations are scrambling, and they assume DEI won't bring in revenue, so they give it the smallest budget. Then they allocate what little DEI money they do have to programs and events concerning hiring rather than retention, professional development, education, or training. That might help bring in new entry-level employees of color, but if you don't dedicate resources to retention and development, how are you going to help advance these workers to executive positions? If you don't give DEI the same dollars that you do to the other departments, if you don't invest in progress, no one is going to suddenly work miracles. Companies want change, but they don't want to line-item a budget around that change.

DEI is just one example. No matter what department you are in, if your budget is small, or small relative to other departments or to the overall revenue, then your team is probably not considered especially valuable. The resources you are allocated will tell you how integral your team is to the overall org chart. On a more personal level, your budget will tell you if you have been trusted to work on something of high value, and if you are considered a vital player in the overall machine. You can be given a fancy title—vice president of this or that—and still not be working on valuable business. I've worked with plenty of companies where I would see someone with a fancy title and be impressed, and then find out they didn't have the ear of management or a workable budget. They'd been at the company a long time, and they were being placated with an impressive title but no real influence.

When you get access to budgets, you get access to information. And information is power. I can't stress enough how important it is to understand the business of where you work. Here are some questions you might start looking into once you can access the budget data: What is the revenue of the company? What is the percentage of your current team's contribution? What is your manager's budget, and how does your team fit into the bigger department? If your team's business went away, how would that impact the company overall? This information can better inform you about raises, about opportunities, about longevity. Is this a company that is invested in you and believes in you, or are you a check-the-box hire who won't be able to get anything done because you'll never get the resources you need? Is this a company that you want to invest your time and skills and energy in, or should you be looking for the next opportunity? Money, as they say, talks.

Be Ready, Stay Ready

Back when I was in grad school, before I even started my full-time career, I was looking for an internship. I wanted to work in PR, and I knew that just applying online into a generic inbox and crossing my fingers wasn't going to cut it. I knew it because I had tried! I wanted to work at Edelman, a top global PR firm, and I'd applied through the website probably a half-dozen times. Nothing. Eventually, I found a specific HR contact and e-mailed her with a note that expressed my interest in PR and my desire to work at Edelman specifically. I ended the note by saying that I would keep applying until I got my foot in the door, and that's when I finally got a response. "Are you free today at three P.M.?" the e-mail said. And I sure was! After the HR rep and I spoke, she asked if I could start Monday. Again, "Yes, ma'am!" I was ready, I stayed ready, and when the opportunity finally presented itself, I jumped on it.

I think about that story a lot these days, because the work climate has changed. I can imagine a job candidate getting that "free at three P.M. today?" request and saying, "No, but I'm free Friday at two." And of course, sometimes you really can't be somewhere at a moment's notice. But that's the kind of gusto and chutzpah and drive and ambition that companies are looking for in employees. Not just when they are hiring, but all the time. Part of doing the work is saying yes and being prepared. If you are the employee who routinely says, "I don't have the bandwidth," or flounders when an assignment comes your way, that's a strike against you before you've even delivered a final product. Opportunities don't always happen on your timeline—they usually won't—so you have to be ready and you have to be ready to act fast, because when the next chance comes your way, you probably won't have a week to decide if it's right for you. You won't necessarily have a window to clear other things off your plate. The chance to lead a project or speak at an important panel or submit yourself for a promotion—these things don't come around every day. Employers want to see that you are always ready. You want the work, and you crave the success. They want to see that you're hungry.

The Meeting before the Meeting

Early in my career, I was working at a small company and there was an issue with payroll. I can't remember the exact details of the problem, but the result was that they would have to pay all employees seven days late. Leadership touched base with everyone at the company to ask if this was okay. If not, they said, they would find another solution. What I remember is that I was young and had to make rent, so I told them the week-late payment wouldn't work for me. A paycheck shouldn't be flexible if you are doing your job, so I asked to get my money on time. Turned out, I was the only one who communicated this. When I spoke up, the executives acted shocked. "Oh, you're the only one who said that," they said. It's hard to believe that in a company with a lot of junior employees who don't make big salaries no one else would express concern or have questions about getting paid a week behind schedule. But clearly there had been conversations behind the scenes. Leadership had quietly gotten everyone else on board so that when they approached the group with their proposal, they knew they would have a majority. And I didn't want to stick out or make waves, so once I heard I was alone in my concerns, I backed off. "Oh, okay, never mind," I said. They got what they wanted.

This is a minor example of "the meeting before the meeting" (though it didn't feel so minor to me at the time). If the leadership at that company had approached everyone at the same time with their late-pay proposal, they would have been met with a million different answers and a million different concerns. People would have had questions. Instead, there was a resounding "No problem!" Leadership quietly got buy-in across the board so that they had their answer before they ever asked the question.

When I talk about the meeting before the meeting, I'm talking about these moments when group decisions are made and agreed upon before any new idea is actually brought to the table. For every decision being made by a group in a conference room, there's a conversation between a smaller group happening behind closed doors. *That's* the meeting before the meeting—where the decision-makers are convening to align on their desired outcomes. A project lead might say they want to gather the team to propose a new campaign, but before that gathering, they will go to various team members to ensure they have their support. No one wants to be surprised or shot down, especially in a group setting. So the person who needs an answer, if they are smart, will have already led individual members toward their side. Conversations are happening behind the scenes so that by the time the big meeting takes place, the person pitching the idea already has buy-in.

Why does this matter? First of all, understanding how decisions get made and how to sell your ideas internally is critical to understanding the business process. Second, once you understand the dynamics of the meeting behind the meeting, you'll be better equipped to assess your own standing in your office and among your colleagues. But let's start with the first part, because doing good work involves moving things forward. There will come a time when you need support or buy-in so that you can get something done—maybe you need team members to agree to your proposed solution to a problem; maybe you want support for a creative idea; maybe you want to work on a certain project—in any of these cases, you have to understand the strategy of organizational decision-making. Whenever you're pitching an idea, you want to know you already have buy-in, because if you can't get it privately, you won't get it publicly.

The meeting before the meeting can be as informal as a conversation in the break room or on Slack. Maybe you mention to a co-worker that you're going to pitch a new campaign in the next team meeting, or that you want to enlist an outside agency to overhaul the company website. Discussing these things ahead of time is a good way to get a pulse check of where your colleagues stand and hopefully get them on board. It also could be an actual meeting, convened in advance, between a smaller subset of colleagues. There are so many decisions that need to get made on a regular basis, and while there are leaders who are responsible for moving things forward and guiding things in the right direction, choices aren't made in isolation. Leaders at all levels—whether they are running an entire organization or department or just a single project—need support, and gathering that support starts early.

It's important that you understand this, because if you have big ideas you want to pitch, you can do all the necessary prep work, you can prepare a flawless presentation, you can plan answers to every question, but if you haven't gotten any support from colleagues ahead of time, you are setting yourself up for failure. Like I said, people don't like to be surprised. They need some time to sit with an idea and come around to any proposed changes. They want to understand how any new procedure or product or service will affect *them*. If you present a roomful of 10 people with an idea for the first time all at once, you will be met with a room full of concerns and probably 10 different reactions. People have a lot of questions when it comes to implementing or launching something new, and those questions will probably take longer to answer than the 10 minutes you allotted at the end of your presentation. Getting buy-in for your idea—in other words, convening the meeting before the meeting—will take time. You will need to dedicate extra hours and extra energy to your prep work so you can explain what's coming to whichever key people you want on your side ahead of time. This will also help you get a sense of what questions will come up during your presentation. If there is someone influential who will be in the meeting—that person who, when they agree, everyone else does too and when they don't, you're dead in the water—you've got to get their support in advance. Maybe that means jumping on a call for 15 minutes or going on a quick Starbucks run a few days in advance. But the purpose of the conversation shouldn't simply be for you to tell them your idea and try to convince them it's great. The goal is for you to share why your proposal will benefit *them*. At the end of the day, if you need someone to vouch for your idea, you need to relate it back to them and explain how it will help them get their work done. At the very least, you need to convince them ahead of time that it won't adversely affect their work or their time, but ideally you are showing them why whatever it is you want to happen will make *their* life easier. Yes, you want them to understand your pitch ahead of time so that the meeting goes more smoothly, but if this person will affect whether or not you get the green light you need, you need to demonstrate how they will be helped by supporting your big idea.

Understanding the meeting before the meeting isn't only about moving your own ideas forward, it's also about inclusion. It's about ensuring that you're a part of the decision-making process and that your input carries weight, and also that you understand what's happening when it doesn't. If someone else is running point on a project, you *want* to be one of the people they consult ahead of time. If getting your support is important, that means you are valued. Being in the meeting before the meeting indicates that you have influence, or that it's important to your leaders that you are on board with the next steps. If you are consistently consulted—either formally or informally—before big changes are introduced, or if you find you're rarely surprised in a meeting because you've always heard about the next idea ahead of time, that's important information. It means you're secure in your job and integral to operations.

But it's likely the case that you won't *always* be in on the behind-the-scenes conversations. There are a couple of reasons for this. It might just be innocent. Maybe you're new to your job, and you haven't yet integrated into the team or your buy-in isn't as vital. Maybe you're consulted on some decisions but not others. But as a person who is eager to succeed and is always thinking about her role, you want to eliminate surprises—or at the very least you want to minimize them—so you can plan ahead and know your next move. You want to know what's coming at each of those big meetings so you aren't blindsided. You want to understand how you're affected and how you can plan accordingly. How can you be sure you're included? To start, if you know that someone is leading a meeting or presentation or internal pitch, volunteer to help them out ahead of time. If you're going to contribute, they'll have to divulge the expected messaging. You can also rely on all those relationships we talked about in the first part of this book. If you weren't invited to the meeting before the meeting, maybe someone you have a good relationship with was. If they want to help you get ahead, they will tell you what you need to know. You will be better equipped because someone is looking out for you. If you know a big meeting is coming up and you don't know what to expect, take accountability. Start asking questions. One of the main reasons we network is for information. Each piece of the puzzle is interconnected—relationships provide information; information helps strengthen relationships. Together, these things build careers.

It's also possible, if you're not a part of the meeting before the meeting, that you've been purposely left out. When someone is pitching a new idea, they don't necessarily need everyone's buy-in beforehand. They just need a majority, and at the very least they need the influencers. Sometimes, they want a few people to disagree, for optics if nothing else. But let me tell you, it's lonely out there on that limb, being the only one with a difference of opinion. If you are consistently boxed out of important conversations, take note. This is a clue to your life span at the company, and your perceived value at the company. Ask yourself: is this a place you want to dedicate your professional energy to? Maybe. It could be that there are just a few bad apples and the organization as a whole deserves your time and effort. You may not need to leave, you may just need to figure out how to become more integral within your department. It could be the push you need to start considering what conversations you should be having so that you feel more included. But it might also be a sign that you'll always be just a number at this company. A seat filler. If you are continually left out of strategic conversations, it could be a sign that you'll want to consider other opportunities. But before you can figure any of that out, you need to simply start paying attention. Where are the meetings before the meetings taking place? Who is a part of them? How are strategic decisions getting made, and are you being offered a voice in those conversations?

How to Spot a No (and Turn It into a Yes)

Success cannot happen in a vacuum. We need other people. For guidance and mentorship and advice and connection, but also for the simple purpose of moving our work forward. We need the go-ahead to move to the next stage in a project. We need a recommendation for a promotion. We need someone to sign off on a budget. Unless you are the CEO of your own company, there will be someone who needs to say yes in order for you to succeed—and even if you *are* the founder and CEO, there will be clients, customers, and a board to answer to. Someone, usually more than one, will need to say yes to ensure your success.

If you are a person who is simply unable to read the room—if you cannot see it when a no is coming down the pike—you will not be able to execute good work or good judgment. You will face more rejection and more bumps in the road than necessary because you won't be able to course-correct ahead of time. Doing the work often means anticipating reactions and then tweaking your actions in order to get the reaction you want and the approval you need. If you can't recognize when a no is coming, you will find yourself bumping up against a wall over and over and over again.

The unfortunate truth is that people don't like to say no. For whatever reason, it makes them feel uncomfortable. Whether it's your manager, a colleague, or a leader in your industry whom you're trying to connect with, they'd usually rather talk around the no—avoiding the topic or distracting from the conversation or even ghosting—than to just say no outright. They think that's the kinder, gentler approach, which, of course, it's not. I wish people would just rip off the Band-Aid and say no when they want to, but more often than not they don't. Maybe this sounds like a good thing—*If people don't like to say no, then I'll get all the yeses I need!* Not exactly. Instead people will kick the can down the road. They'll avoid a decision altogether, leaving you paralyzed while you wait for an answer or, worse, giving you hope when there is no hope in sight. Or, they'll wait until the absolute last minute, allowing you to spend plenty of time and energy on something they were never going to agree to in the first place. Sometimes they'll even tell a lie or make up an excuse in order to avoid saying those two little letters.

I've come up against this countless times in my career. In my first job, none of my higher-ups wanted to tell me that I wasn't executing to their expectations. When I asked if I was doing a good job, I was told that, sure, everything was great. It wasn't until it was too late that I learned the truth. I've worked in situations where I thought I was going to get a promotion, but then instead of saying no to me directly, my boss said no behind the scenes, essentially ripping the opportunity out from under me. Even as a founder of my own company, I've witnessed super-successful, executive-level leaders work too hard to avoid saying no.

Take, for example, a national leader in the finance industry who we have invited numerous times to speak at ColorComm events. Every year we've asked her to speak at one conference or another, and every year we've gotten the run around. Finally, when our 10-year-anniversary event rolled around in 2021, we thought this would be the moment. We put out the ask, and she connected us with her chief of staff so they could learn more. If you are trying to work with someone and they pawn you off to their chief of staff before you've ever spoken to them directly, that's a bad sign. Then the chief of staff referred us to one of *her* reports—another bad sign! At this point we were going to have to convince someone two levels below our intended speaker that we were worth her time, and we also had to trust that the information we relayed to this employee would get properly translated up through two tiers of the organization. That's too much opportunity for error and communication breakdown. At this point, I knew that what we had was basically an informational call dressed up as actual consideration of our request. I was talking to someone too far removed, and it was obvious that this company took the call so they could say that they did the right thing. In the end, we were told that this would-be speaker couldn't join us at the anniversary event because of COVID concerns. Fine, understandable. Except a couple of weeks before the event—after she'd already declined our invitation with the COVID excuse—I saw this same woman, in the flesh, at a Met Gala after-party. We just stared at each other, both shocked. I'm sure her team assumed we wouldn't run in the same circles. Oops! She should have just said no from the beginning—this was a seasoned leader with a national profile, and I was sad to see that this Black woman was unable to show up to a 10th-anniversary luncheon celebrating the work of advancing women of color. But if she had simply said she didn't have the bandwidth, it would have been believable. And it would have been much less awkward when we ran into each other. (It's a good lesson for when *you* are in the position of needing to give a no. When you do so, be gracious, but also be mindful of your excuse. You can get in trouble if you make up excuses and then get caught.)

If you can develop the ability to spot a no coming—the indicators are usually there—you can save yourself a lot of effort and unnecessary work and shift your focus to an approach that will produce a yes, now or in the future. To start, decide in advance how many follow-ups you think a specific person might need. Three is standard—research shows that three follow-up e-mails, for example, bring the highest response rate—but at particularly busy times of year you can bump that up to five. But no more. If you've tried three to five times to get an answer from someone and you aren't getting a yes *or* a no? Move on. Stall tactics and unresponsiveness are major clues. If you've asked for a promotion and you're told time and again that it will happen "soon," maybe next quarter, or if every time you ask one specific question your boss suddenly stops responding, take that as a hint. I had a mentee who worked in advertising doing all the right things—she put in time after hours, she had a fast response time when clients or colleagues reached out, she never missed a deadline—but they kept dangling a promotion in front of her without offering any specifics. It would happen toward the end of the year, they said, and then the top of the year. Suddenly it was spring, a year later than the original promotion trajectory, and nothing. It was time to accept that a no was coming—or maybe it had already come, if not in so many ways.

If you reach out to someone with an ask and they don't request more information, that's another sign. Sometimes you'll follow up—"Is there anything else I can provide to help you make your decision?"—and someone you've barely spoken to will say, "Nope, I've got all I need." How is that possible? There's always more. The first attempt can't possibly encapsulate every piece of information that is available about every request. So if someone doesn't care for more information, they probably just don't care. If your request is kicked to another person, and then another and another, that's another hint. The truth is, the signs are almost always there and they are usually pretty obvious, but we get hopeful for the yes so we ignore the red flags or come up with reasons why this time is an exception. And listen, I'm not trying to be the buzzkill. I just don't want you sitting there in a fog, thinking you're going to get your project green-lit or be able to take on this new initiative or get to go to that conference when it's not going to happen. I want you to pay attention and understand the signs so that you don't waste your time or energy and instead can pivot faster to paths that will produce the answer you want. Because a no doesn't always mean no forever—if you do the work and play the game, a no today can turn into a yes down the road.

— 7 —

YOU NEED . . .
TO MANAGE PERSONAL
RELATIONSHIPS IN YOUR
PROFESSIONAL WORLD

In 2021, a friend came to me and pitched the idea for a new initiative—a series of online panels for the modern professional woman, which we would host together. It was a way to mentor and give back, she said. A way to share our expertise with the world. This friend was, like me, a successful professional woman of color. As she explained her idea and got me on board, we started getting down to brass tacks. We wouldn't charge anyone to sit in on the conversations, but eventually we'd hope to get sponsors. At first it seemed like a good idea. Here were two ambitious and accomplished Black women sharing their experience, professional wisdom, and lessons learned with other ambitious professional women. The problem, I quickly learned, is that partnering with friends often starts from a place of emotion rather than strategy. We wanted to do something exciting together, so we just forged ahead without thinking big-picture. Deep down we both knew that mixing business with friendship can be risky, so we didn't focus very much on the business side of things. We didn't come up with a business plan or even a long-term vision. Do what you love and the money will follow, right? Not exactly.

Looking back, I can see that I was afraid to say no to my friend, and that came back to bite me. When a friend comes to you excited about a big idea, it's hard to respond with anything but a resounding yes. I wanted to support her, so I forgot to ask the questions that I would have asked if any other potential business partner had approached me for a partnership. Questions like: What are the business goals? Where do we see this initiative in a year? What need or void in the market are we filling? What will we do differently than other similar offerings out there? We talked about our tactical goals—spoke every Wednesday to mentees to shed light on our careers and give advice—but the business strategy conversation never happened. And eventually, a week or two after our launch, it hit me: I already do this work. It's called ColorComm. I wasn't always the one speaking on the ColorComm platform or at our events, but the work and the content were pretty similar. When I had time to actually think about this new endeavor, I couldn't quite identify why I was doing it. Because I believed in the idea, or because I didn't want to let down a friend?

From the get-go, my friend and I had a difficult time. We had calls with our teams and realized we weren't see-ing eye-to-eye on how to execute the work or what our priorities should be. It's obvious to me now that we should have had these discussions before we ever agreed to work together. In fact, when you're doing business with friends you should be even *more* deliberate about discussing strat-egy and outlining clear goals and business practices. I didn't want to risk the relationship by having these hard conversations or seeming unsupportive, so in the end I said yes . . . and our friendship was still affected.

Navigating personal relationships in a professional world is complicated. Getting into business with friends is risky and can jeopardize the relationship, and becoming *too* friendly with a business connection, well, same thing. In this world of constant collaborations and cross-brand partnerships, opportunities to work with friends pop up everywhere. If you're not smart about these partnerships, you can end up tanking the business *and* the friendship. As tempting as it might be to collaborate so you can both get ahead, your first concern should be the viability of the endeavor. Even if you think it will help out your friend, you have to remember: you're not responsible for the growth of your peers.

Relationships are tricky and always changing. Successfully climbing the professional ladder is just one more variable that can make them that much more complicated. Knowing how to hold the boundaries between your personal life and your professional life isn't just about getting ahead, it's about maintaining some joy while you do so. It's about keeping your relationships intact on both sides of the line. Conquering your career can feel like a lonely business, so you'll need your people by your side—at home and at work.

How Friendly Is Too Friendly?

Part of building closeness in real-life friendships is being vulnerable. When we open up to our friends and share our struggles or our fears, we connect on a deeper level than if we just talked about TV or hobbies or what we did over the weekend. But when it comes to work friendships, keeping the connection close to the surface is perfectly fine. Professional relationships should always be just that—professional. Yes, your colleagues should know you on a personal level, but by "personal" I mean that they should know that you're a cyclist, or that you love to read, or that you're an avid traveler. They should want to chat with you at the watercooler about *Abbott Elementary* or the NCAA tournament—they should not, necessarily, know your entire dating history or family drama.

You want your co-workers to feel like they know your personality and like they've had friendly conversations with you. That they "know" you. The intention of a work connection is that the other person will vouch for you within the company or speak your name when you're not in the room. It's also about building rapport so that you can work well together and produce good results. You want to find common ground so you feel free to pass assignments back and forth. And you also want to build trust. Whether it's with your employees or your co-workers or your managers, trust is what will motivate these people to have your back on days when you might be underperforming or distracted by stuff going on in your personal life. After all, we aren't robots. None of us can be executing at our usual level of excellence every single day. If you've established a track record of responsibility and camaraderie and collaboration with the workers around you, you will earn leeway for the times when you're going through a rough patch or not producing at your usual capacity. People will give you more grace when they know that you're someone who delivers, and someone with whom they already feel connected.

But all that means your connection must be one of mutual respect. It requires letting your colleagues in enough to see that you are a person underneath your "colleague" hat, one who enjoys similar activities or listens to similar podcasts or eats similar food—but not so much that they have a front-row seat to any messiness you have going on in your life. Keep your private life private. The decisions you make in your personal life, if you broadcast them, will affect how you are perceived in your work life—and this is especially true if you are one of very few women of color at the office. If you are already othered, people are more likely to generalize and assume that a small problem in one area means you have problems in all areas. You start talking about the challenges you have with dating? Your colleagues might very well equate it, if only subconsciously, to challenges in your work life. You've got to be selective about what you share, especially if you're new to your job or your company. Over time, your colleagues will learn about your life at home. If you've been at a company for 5, 10, 20 years, people will know about the big things. You might get engaged or married in that time, you could have kids or get a divorce. You might lose a loved one or have to deal with health issues. These are big life events and your colleagues will find out, for better and for worse. But if you are broadcasting all the drama of your divorce and trying to talk through your issues with everyone seated around the conference table—that's what therapy is for. And do not showcase misbehavior—whether it's getting drunk, getting flirty, or anything else you might do during a night on the town. That's what girls' nights are for. When you are out with colleagues, keep it classy. Even if you have developed nice friendships with your co-workers, they don't need to see your messy side. You need to maintain their respect, which doesn't include being the subject of office gossip the next day. There is still a level of competition to this environment. There are only so many people who can get ahead. You want to be one of those people, and you don't need anything from your personal life popping up to work against you.

Remember, even if you become very friendly with your employees and colleagues, they are still employees and colleagues. Those titles don't change. The vast majority of the time, these people didn't enter your life as friends and they aren't going to exit as friends. They are co-workers, and at the end of the day, this is still work. That's true even if this is your going-away party and you think you will never see these people again, or if you're just out with employees from a different department and you think you'll never really work together. Industries overlap; people move around. Most organizations have employees across marketing, diversity and inclusion, engineering, sales, IT, finance—you never know who might suddenly be your co-worker in your next workplace. Remember, people ebb and flow, but your reputation will follow you wherever you land.

To that end, please, please, *please* pay attention to your social media feeds. We live in a world of oversharing, but remember that if something is online, your co-workers and managers and employees can probably see it. Be selective about what you post. Be mindful of who is following you on each platform, but also remember that if your profile is public, anyone can see it. Don't assume that because your boss doesn't follow you, they don't see your content. People make fake accounts so they can monitor employees without you knowing it's them. They sign in under friends' accounts. They hear from other folks at the office if something especially noteworthy is posted online. Don't showcase your messy weekend, and don't complain about your job—if you don't want someone at work to see it, make your life easier and do not post it.

It's Lonely at the Top

Office friendships are largely circumstantial. If you change jobs, these relationships often die out. You might have the occasional catch-up dinner, and if you both stay in the same industry you may connect over drinks at a conference, but the daily connection that was once there will probably go away. That's to be expected and usually isn't awkward or uncomfortable. What *can* be a bit tense is if one of you starts climbing the ranks faster than the other. I used to regularly go to work events with one specific professional friend. We often saw each other at panels or happy hours and we realized that we both usually attended alone, so we decided to travel as a pair. We were together a lot—and it became one of those things where if someone saw one of us at an industry event they would ask about the other. But as time passed, our careers took different paths. Now I'm sometimes in spaces where she isn't, and that has caused some awkwardness. Our relationship is more strained than it once was.

Careers advance at different speeds. You might start out together as assistants, and for any number of reasons—whether it's merit, or connections, or luck—one gets promoted quickly while the other has to tread water a bit longer. This can absolutely result in resentment or jealousy. I wish it wasn't the case, but if it's true that nothing worth having is easy, relationships are at the top of that list.

I tell you all this because I want you to understand the requirements of a professional friendship as your star begins to rise. Mutual respect is paramount. Treating people with kindness, absolutely. But as you are establishing yourself in your industry and your career, you are not responsible for anyone's success but your own. Yes, once you find success, the hope is that as a woman of color you will help clear the way for those who will come after you. You will create more seats at the table and advocate for those who can't advocate for themselves. We absolutely need to pave the way in order to increase opportunity and equity for future generations in the spaces where we work. We have to give as we receive. But as you are climbing the ladder, it's not your job to help up everyone around you. You cannot pull someone else to the next rung while simultaneously trying to hang on yourself. You cannot take responsibility for someone else's career or ensure that your colleagues get the same opportunities as you. So, when you are offered a seat at the table, if the offer is extended privately, do not ask for a plus one. And I'm not talking about a figurative seat at a figurative table. I'm talking about a real invite, to a dinner or a party or an exclusive industry event. You might feel loyal to a colleague who shares an office or a boss with you. You might feel guilty if you are elbowing your way into spaces without them, so you figure you'll just ask the organizer if you can bring a friend. No big deal. I know you're doing this to be a good pal and colleague, but I'm telling you: the organizer is taking a mental note. I know this because one of my biggest pet peeves as the CEO of a company that throws high-end industry events, is when invited guests ask me if they can bring other people. Sometimes they just assume they can and show up with a friend in tow; other times they send a note asking permission, but usually that note assumes it's fine. It will say something like "Hey! Just confirming that it's okay if I bring [insert friend's name here] to the event as my guest? Thanks so much!" But here's the thing: let's say we only have 100 seats for a luncheon. If everyone brought a plus-one, that would double the size of the event. That's twice as much space, twice as much food and drink. There are costs associated with each person in the room. People assume that we would be happy to have their friend in attendance, but the reality is that if we wanted that person at our event, we would have invited them. So, as much as you wish you could bring your friend or colleague along as you get more invites or get included in new spaces, don't sacrifice future invitations from the organizer by asking that an uninvited friend be included at an event. Don't jeopardize your hard-earned opportunities in order to vouch for someone else. Before you ask if you can bring someone, ask yourself: Will this person service the needs of the organizer? Is she a celebrity? A household name? Someone the organizer would be over the moon to have? And if so, why didn't they think of inviting this person in the first place? You need to have a really good reason for asking to add another person's name to the guest list. If you are trying to bring someone along just because she is your work wife, that's not a good enough reason.

Confidence Is the Best Accessory

Here's a little secret I've learned over the years as I've attended more and more events, many of which have increasingly smaller guest lists: as much as success relies on relationships, you also have to be comfortable and confident being alone. Maybe you'd never go to a party alone in your personal life. Maybe you always want to make an entrance with a date on your arm or a friend at your side, or you want to know who's going to be there before you commit. But let me tell you, when it comes to professional events, the rules of your social life do not apply. I was recently invited to a notable CEO's home in California. The invitation was for me only—I was not invited with a guest. I was not told who else would be in attendance. All I was told was the name of the event, the address, and that there was a no-photo policy. I could tell immediately that it was going to be an event full of power players, and I wanted to be in the room. These are the kinds of rooms where new connections are made, where the first sparks of a business deal are mentioned over passed hors d'oeuvres. I knew this was a career opportunity, and you can bet I didn't ask who was going to be there when I RSVP'd. I didn't worry if I would have friends in the room or if I could bring a plus-one. I didn't ask questions; I just showed up with gratitude for the invite and figured I would know people. It was a stunning event at a beautiful home in Los Angeles. And guess what? I knew 75 percent of the people in the room. When you get an invitation to any career event, you have to have the confidence that even if you go in blind, not knowing a soul, you will find your way. In fact, sometimes you should *want* to go alone, because the friend or colleague you bring along might have an agenda that doesn't align with yours. Don't let not knowing anyone or going somewhere alone deter you. If you are savvy enough to get a spot in the room, you can work the room.

Another rule from your social life that you can forget right now: showing up "fashionably late." If you hate arriving before the party is underway because you don't want to awkwardly mingle or you want to make an entrance, fine. On your own time, you do you. But when it comes to professional events, if the start time calls for 6 P.M., be there a half hour earlier.

A couple of years ago, one of my mentors invited me to a small private toast to honor and celebrate Kimberly Godwin, the president of ABC News. The event started at 7 P.M. I got to the building at 7:05 P.M. I thought I was early! In fact, I worried that I was too early, and that I'd have to go somewhere to kill time so I wasn't the only person in the room. But since I was there I figured I'd pop in and take a peek at the scene. At five after seven, the room was nearly full! Standing around and chitchatting were Gayle King, Robin Roberts, Al Roker, Tamron Hall, and a number of TV executives. The heavyweights of media heavyweights. These are people I wanted to talk to, to get to know better. It was an important business opportunity for me to be in that space. After all, I work in media and communications—I often ask these people to contribute time to ColorComm as speakers or mentors or panelists. And for them, 7 P.M. is late—they are morning anchors! Their alarm is going off at 3 or 4 A.M.

A friend of mine who lived in Washington, D.C., was also invited. She showed up at 8:30 P.M., and the room was half empty. She was shocked. "In D.C., events start late," she said. "Well, in New York," I told her, "they start on time." If I had waited to enter the room until I could walk in with a friend or I had killed time nearby so I wouldn't be one of the "first" people there, I would have missed the important connections that I was able to foster that day.

You never lose anything by being on time. You can always leave an event early, but if you arrive late you'll never know who and what you missed. When events are work related, people don't want to be there all night. They want to get home to their families. They want to kick off their heels and relax in front of the TV. People stroll into events late because they want to look cool or busy and they don't want to look desperate, but I promise, no one is looking at you.

The other thing about that event? I had no idea that the Gayle Kings and Tamron Halls of the world were going to be there. My mentor didn't tell me. But she told me it was going to be a good business opportunity, so I showed up. Trust the person inviting you. Have the confidence to know that if you were invited into the room, you deserve to be there, and you can walk in, on your own, with your head held high. If you don't question if you belong, no one else should, either.

Personal Friends, Professional Success

Climbing the professional ladder can feel lonely. Relationships you make in your professional life are not generally rooted in authenticity, they are based on an exchange of information and opportunity, and they prosper only as long as those exchanges continue. There's nothing wrong with that—it's the name of the game—but we all need real, true friendships as well. The people who knew you when, the people who will be your shoulders to cry on and your cheerleaders and who will have your back when you want to vent about a colleague or a business deal gone wrong—they are crucial to maintaining your sanity in a professional world that is especially hard on women of color. We need the support of the people who see us and love us for exactly who we are, which is why it's so important that we respect those relationships and don't let our professional success muddle things up.

Soon after I started ColorComm, an article was written about me and my business. It was in *Black Enterprise*. I sent it to everyone I knew. More press followed: a spot on the local news, national press, and lifestyle press. Each time it was the biggest deal ever. And each time, I sent the clip around to all my friends—I was so excited, how could I not? But then there was something in *The Washington Post*, and that was an even bigger deal! Every time I got a piece of news coverage I thought, *This is it. This is the pinnacle. I will never get something like this again!* And so, like clockwork, I forwarded the accolades to my friends and family. Each and every time.

I like to think that with time and maturity I realized I needed to pull it back, but I probably had friends who hinted that, okay, it's a lot. Here I was in my bubble thinking, *I worked so hard! We've been hustling, and it's finally paying off!* To me, it seemed like each clip was something different—this article was highlighting a new initiative, that one was about an anniversary—but at the end of the day, to people who don't work in my industry, it felt like a little much. They started wondering, how many times can we pat you on the back?

As you get more shine, there can be a feeling that it never ends: *We thought this was your big moment? Oh wait, now* this *is your big moment?* While your friends want to support your success, they may feel like they've done the cheerleading already. And if they're not advancing at the same pace, or if they're in an industry where the work is simply not as celebrated and doesn't involve as many public kudos, celebrating someone else can start to feel exhausting. If you are the one getting the constant claps, choose the highlights and share those. Be mindful of how your constant self-promotion might come off to your friends. If you are getting coverage all the time, at some point, that is just what you do. It's no longer a kudos or a clap, it's just your job. So pay attention to the information you disseminate among your friends, and understand that success comes with power—in this case, the power to make others feel insecure or frustrated about their own careers if they aren't advancing at the same pace. Remember, not everyone needs every little detail, and sometimes too much is just too much.

And if you're the friend receiving all the notifications about X recognition or Y success? If your work moves at a different pace and it's starting to wear you down? It's okay to cheerlead from a distance. You want to be supportive of your friends, but you don't have to read every article they send or comment on every social post or be super invested in their professional life. The hope is that your friendship is independent of your respective careers, so while of course I know you will root for your friend's success, you don't need to respond every time there is another alert. That said, if yours is the quieter career, absolutely share when something happens that you are proud of. This is your time!

I shared all those kudos when ColorComm first started because I was so eager to show my family and friends the result of our hard work. But I've been the person getting the constant e-mails from a friend alerting me to yet another one of her achievements. I have a friend who is a buzzed-about Black lawyer, and she is often getting press mentions or social media shout-outs or spots on TV. And I've got to say, she's exhausting. I am exhausted. She is always getting featured in some outlet or another, and I cannot keep up with the congratulations. I'm sure she feels the same way I did—that she's been hustling forever and she's finally getting her due and wants her friends to celebrate with her. And of course I'm happy for her. I want her to succeed. I want to celebrate my friends. I want to celebrate women of color even if they aren't my friends! But her constant notifications were a helpful reminder that what is just pride or excitement for one person can come off more like narcissism to the people on the other end. Not to mention, for people who aren't in your professional world, all the different recognitions start to blend together. All the different lawyer shout-outs sound the same to someone in PR or tech. So don't get mad if your kudos from friends start to trickle off. I've seen people rise professionally and then get mad as the chorus of applause in their personal life got quieter. They chalked it up to jealousy rather than acknowledging that their personal friends were more interested in being a part of their personal lives than cheerleaders for their professional success.

The other thing people don't need to be constantly reminded of? How busy you are. When you are prioritizing work and career, your calendar can feel pretty full. Your friends try to make plans with you, but there's always a reason you can't make it—you're traveling for work or you have an evening event or you're prepping for a big presentation. But remember, just because you might be the one who is killing it in your friend group, that doesn't mean everything revolves around you and your work schedule. If someone proposes a group dinner on Thursday, you don't need to explain all the reasons you can't attend. If every time you're invited somewhere you explain all the reasons why you are too busy, you'll become a real eye roll. *She's sooooo important, we get it.* Just tell your friends what night works for you, and remember that you are just one person in a group of people who are all busy, who all have other stuff going on in their lives.

The point of all this is simple: pay attention to how your work talk comes off to your friends. Of course you can and should share your big career moments with them— the good and the bad—but good friendships transcend work. The more your career builds, the more the people in your professional life will need things from you and demand your attention. And if you're a woman of color, especially one who is working in a predominatly white office or industry, playing the game and being "on" all the time can be so tiring. Without a good support system, playing the professional game can be a lot. I want you to enjoy the journey, and that means holding on to friendships that provide you with some relief from the grind. You will need the people who know and appreciate the real you—not the one who is always buttoned up and on her A game, but the person you are when your defenses are down and you can breathe a sigh of relief. These are the people who knew you before you became whoever you are today, and if your professional life hits a bump in the road, they are the ones who will be with you after.

Money Matters

I have a good friend who found career success pretty quickly out of college; while the rest of us were hustling, she seemed to be rolling in dough. Or at least it seemed that way to us, because she always picked up the tab. We'd have a girls' night on the town and she was generous with her earnings, grabbing the check before any of us had a chance to contribute. The problem came when one night we went out and she *didn't* feel like paying. By the time the bill came she was stuck with it because a bunch of folks had already gone home and assumed she was taking care of it. She had created expectations, and then she felt resentful and used. It sucked for everyone involved.

Money is a complicated topic. When you're part of a group of friends who work across different industries, everyone's financial state will be different. One person might be living in the lap of luxury while another is pinching pennies, and this can cause conflict. There is friction when one person suggests a group activity that someone else can't afford, and there's a similar reaction if people assume their more successful friend will cover costs for all socializing. But one thing I've seen with women of color especially is that when we find financial success, we want to bankroll activities or cover expenses for our friends. Women of color are more likely to be the first in their family to work in white-collar professions, and they are less likely to come from a background of financial wealth. When you aren't used to acquiring wealth and you haven't been taught how to manage it, you are more likely to spend money when you have it. So as women of color start to rise and make more money, they're inclined to start treating their girls to dinners or lunches, they pay for a table at a new hip lounge or cover the alcohol costs for an evening. It comes from a good place—a place of generosity and of understanding that maybe a friend can't play in the same sandbox without a little bit of help. They want to shower those who have been good to them with love. But as happened with my friend, this type of generosity can set a precedent and expectation and dependency that doesn't serve anyone, and frankly makes things trickier than if it had never been offered in the first place.

Finances are a long game. When you first get that big paycheck or you get a raise or a promotion—or if you're adding additional income streams and getting paid to be a speaker or a contributor to an outside organization—it might feel like the money is burning a hole in your pocket. But your financial state may fluctuate. No job is a sure thing, and you don't want to screw yourself later because you couldn't resist flaunting your success the moment you got it. When you make more money, remember that the purpose of your improved finances is not to help everyone who has ever been good to you. If you are going to take care of people on the regular, you are going to drain your finances fast.

Mixing Business with Pleasure

I'm not here to tell you that you should never do business with friends. If the people you know can help you get ahead, I say go after it. It's what rich white men have been doing forever. Whatever industry you work in, if you can call on your network to get business done faster, you absolutely should. And your friends will, and should, do the same. If they need to do business with someone in your industry and they can either ask a total stranger or they can ask you, of course they will come to you first. It's just easier to reach out to someone that you at least know will respond to your e-mail than it is to try to pitch someone you've never met or interacted with. If you can skip the introductions and the backstory, you save a lot of time. But it's not just about ease. People also want to work with their friends because they want to give them business. They want to help them out, give them shine, give them a platform. When it works out, it's a win-win.

Still, any business partnership comes with risks, and the stakes are higher when you work with friends simply because there is more to lose. Don't feel obligated to say yes just because the request comes from a close pal. Do not say, "That's a great idea!" simply because you think it's what she wants to hear. I touched earlier on some of the questions I should have asked before I went into business with my friend. Some other things you need to know before agreeing to work with friends: Is this a business/ project that is going to bring in revenue or is it a hobby? If the former, there will be questions you need answered about ownership, equity, legal, and more. If the latter, do you have goals to bring in money eventually? How much will it cost? You also need to understand each other's working styles. Is one of you a micromanager? Does one of you prefer to fly by the seat of her pants? Do you have the same goals and objectives? Does your friend fill a void in your working style? Do you fill a void in hers? That's what makes a partnership—if you have the same skill set, why would you need to work together? These are the questions I didn't ask during that business venture, and it affected our output. If my friend and I had sat down and discussed all this, we likely would have come to a no together and saved everyone a lot of time and a lot of pain. We would have realized that it wasn't the best time to take on a new project, and it wasn't the best use of our resources. We could always do another deal together when it made more sense and success was more likely. With our project, attendance at our "conversations" decreased every week. We were spending our free time talking to people who weren't that interested, or at least weren't telling their friends. It stopped being worth it.

Of course, not all business with friends is about two people coming together and starting something new. No matter how you and a friend work together, there are risks. Maybe you are considering hiring a friend at your company or recommending a friend for an open position. Maybe you are considering recommending the firm that a friend works at for marketing or PR or graphic design needs. Maybe you are hosting a conference and decide to recruit a friend as one of the speakers because she could use a profile boost. This is exactly what happened to me a couple of years ago at the ColorComm conference. A friend of mine who was a successful professional was interested in speaking. I wouldn't let just anyone present—this is my company's premier conference, after all—but this woman had insight to offer to our audience so I agreed. Before the event, I asked her if she would require airfare or a speaking fee or a hotel room, but she said she only needed a hotel. The rest she would handle herself.

During the time leading up to her speaking engagement, my friend's financial circumstances changed. The week of the conference, her business manager came to us with a whole list of new demands: first-class airfare, hair and makeup—all things we hadn't agreed to and frankly we couldn't accommodate. Had she asked for some of it earlier, maybe we would have been able to help, but at this point our budget had been set for months. We had put a contract in place, but because we were friends, she didn't expect me to hold her to the agreement. I, on the other hand, thought that since we were friends she should understand that I was managing my biggest event of the year, and what she was asking for was inappropriate. We didn't see eye to eye. She did end up speaking at the event without her required expenses covered, and while we are still friends, the incident added challenges to our relationship.

The takeaway from that experience was a clear one, and I can't stress its importance enough: when doing business with friends, the agreement needs to be ironclad. The terms need to be crystal clear. The more you leave open to interpretation, the more one party will make assumptions based on friendship rather than business. It can feel awkward to create formal agreements between friends. This is someone you trust, so a verbal agreement might feel more natural, but that's not how business works. The minute you decide to work together, you should each be clear and upfront about your needs and address them all during the negotiation phase. Don't leave room for shades of gray. That doesn't mean you have to act like strangers or suddenly put your friendship on the back burner. Instead, be honest. Explain that you're asking for more clarity *because* the friendship is so important to you. "I really want to work with you," you might say, "but let's discuss what will happen if this doesn't work out? How we will move forward in our friendship? Can we make a pact that we will always speak kindly to each other?" You want to ask, explicitly, if this doesn't work out, what will that look like? Sometimes we avoid these conversations because we don't want our friends to think we don't believe in them, but it's always better to discuss contingency plans before you need them.

I recently hosted an event with journalist and CNN anchor Abby. It was called the Politics & Inclusion Dinner, and we threw it on the eve of the White House Correspondents' Dinner. In attendance were media leaders of color from across networks and outlets. Abby and I are friends—not necessarily lifelong pals, but we've known each other for a long time—and the reason the event was such a hit was that we both stayed in our lanes. I handled the business partnerships; she brought out the talent. As a business owner, I know how to throw a successful event. She was able to use her relationships to get people to attend. We came to the table with different skills, and as a result the event was a huge success. And, even more important, our friendship remains strongly intact.

At the end of the day, that's what matters. There will always be new business opportunities. If you say no to one deal, another will come along. But you can't replace a friend. Sure you will make new ones, but the people who have known you outside the office, maybe since before your career even started, those relationships can't just be replaced. If you establish a business partnership with someone you don't know outside the working world and things go south, there is often more room for grace. There wasn't a preexisting relationship and people come to business deals with the understanding that things might not work out. When you do business with friends and the business goes south, oftentimes the relationship takes a nose-dive right alongside it. All business should be executed strategically, but if you're working with friends, everything should be handled with a little extra care.

PART THREE

Forging Your Future

— 8 —

YOU NEED . . .
TO COMBAT BURNOUT

It's no secret that burnout—that special category of work exhaustion that causes someone to feel unmotivated, worn down, and unsure how to move forward—is on the rise. Even before the COVID-19 pandemic, burnout was a hot topic of discussion. In January 2019, cultural critic Anne Helen Petersen wrote a viral essay about millennial burnout that eventually turned into her critically acclaimed book *Can't Even*. But for women of color, the content of the essay was nothing new. We have been dealing with the exhaustion of working more than our fair share since—well, since we started working.

The World Health Organization (WHO) defines professional burnout as "a syndrome resulting from workplace stress that has not been successfully managed." WHO characterizes burnout by three factors: feelings of energy depletion or exhaustion, increased mental distance from one's job or feelings of negativism or cynicism related to one's job, and reduced professional efficacy. In other words: you're wiped out, frustrated, and detached from your workplace, and less efficient as a result. As women of color, we've been there—it's a lot harder to stay engaged, energetic, and productive in a workplace where you don't feel supported or you're shouldering the burden of representing an entire race or you're dealing with microaggressions on a daily basis. Recent studies clearly show that women of color are more afflicted by burnout than their male or white female counterparts. In 2018 and 2019, two professors at Harvard Business School (HBS) surveyed HBS graduates working full-time across a variety of fields. Keep in mind, these are people who went to Harvard, which means they already entered the working world with some level of privilege and connection—if nothing else, they had the privilege of having Harvard on their résumé and the connections that an Ivy League education can afford you. Still, they found that "while 17% of all respondents said that they often or very often experienced burnout, a quarter of women said they did. The proportion neared 30% when we looked at women of color. (The proportion of white women reporting this level of burnout was about 23%—notably lower than women of color but still higher than nearly all men.) In fact, more than 30% of Latinas, Black women, and South Asian women said they felt burned out often or very often."[1] That was just one study, but plenty of other research backs it up: women of color are more likely to experience professional burnout than any other group. And the pandemic only made it worse. Burnout increased across the board, but in higher numbers for women than men, and higher numbers for women of color than white women. Burnout during the pandemic got so bad that, according to the *Women in the Workplace* study, "35% of white women [were] planning to leave their job in the next three to six months, as [were] 46% of women of color."[2] In fact, so many workers quit jobs starting in early 2021—often citing burnout and similar issues as the reason—that economic experts gave the trend a name: the Great Resignation.

Burnout is real, and we've all probably felt it. Maybe you're feeling it as you read these pages. If you haven't experienced it, well, I hate to be a downer, but it's likely that you will. All of which is to say, if you want to forge a successful professional future, you need to be able to conquer burnout (or at least manage it) before it conquers you. It starts with figuring out your *why*. Before you quit your job or find a new one or accept this exhaustion as a way of life, ask yourself: *Why* are you burned out? There are so many factors that contribute to burnout, but once you can identify the root of your exhaustion, you can begin to understand what you need to address it, get ahead of it, and keep moving forward.

Sick and Tired of Being Sick and Tired

It's no big surprise that burnout affects women of color more than any other group. All the extra effort it takes to do the "extracurricular" work I've outlined in these pages—the building relationships and communicating your value and taking risks and building a network—is tiring, and it's especially tiring if you're doing it completely on your own. Before women of color even walk in the door of our workplace, we are expected to assimilate and make ourselves fit in in spaces where we naturally stick out. We don't show up looking like the majority, so we have to do a lot of homework from the beginning in order to arrive ready to connect with our colleagues. And those connections are rarely a reciprocal endeavor. Women of color are almost always expected to initiate and execute the work of developing professional friendships—the folks in the majority rarely seek out the one person in the minority group in an effort to connect. The onus is on us to approach our colleagues in the majority and extend an introduction or attempt a connection.

And then there's the matter of actually doing the work. I always say it's a wonder that any group of people can get any work done at all when everyone comes from different backgrounds, different financial statuses, different political backgrounds, different geographic upbringings. That's a lot of differences for any two employees to overcome even in the best of circumstances. Add microaggressions to that list, and sometimes outright racism, and it makes the job even harder. It makes it harder to even want to do the job at all. Those obstacles don't necessarily pop up every day, but they might. You might feel like you're working twice as hard as everyone else just to help others understand you, to help them feel comfortable coming to you for work or even feel comfortable addressing you directly. It can feel like you are constantly teaching in addition to getting the actual work done that's required for your job. Then there's the work of navigating *how* to communicate to your colleague that his or her questions are offensive or make you feel othered. This is tricky and it can feel like a lose-lose: either have a conversation with your colleague that's uncomfortable and could likely result in them being offended or acting like you're unreasonable, or continue to suffer disrespect and microaggressions.

As more attention is paid to DEI work, the hope is that professional diversity trainings will educate your colleagues on your behalf so that they know better than to ask questions that specifically call attention to differences or make someone feel "less than," but those changes can be slow going. I hope it goes without saying that the fact that workplaces are focusing more on DEI issues is a good thing. A focus on increasing recruitment, engagement, and retention of workers of color is long-overdue. Education for all employees to ensure that hiring biases and workplace microaggressions are acknowledged and mitigated is clearly necessary. But in the current professional climate, where organizations want to do better on issues of equity but don't always know where to start, there is a huge burden being placed on people of color to step up and lead the charge for change. Even if you weren't doing diversity work before—if you've *never* done it, if your expertise is in finance or marketing or fundraising—your office may ask you to lead the committee or organize the training, and suddenly instead of easing your burnout, your company's DEI efforts are only adding to it. This is something we hear about at ColorComm all the time: women of color are called on to fix the racial disparities in their companies, and it's a huge and exhausting undertaking, especially because it's ultimately not the people of color who will create the change. The workers in the majority groups, and the leaders in power—those are the people who will foster change. Everyone else can support the effort, but it's the power players who will be calling the shots. It shouldn't be incumbent upon workers of color (and, let's be clear, it's more often women of color, because "housekeeping" roles—like running committees—usually go to women) to resolve the problems that we certainly didn't create.

Are You Burned Out? Or Just Working Hard?

Not every moment of fatigue or stress or frustration or unhappiness is a moment of burnout. Understanding and identifying the difference is important because we all go through cycles at work. We all feel annoyed sometimes. We all have bad days. You don't want to walk away from a good thing because you've misidentified regular work stress as never-ending burnout. On the flip side, you don't want to sit in a bad case of burnout because you assume it's normal stress. When you find yourself thinking you're in the throes of burnout, ask yourself: Do you always feel like a hamster on a wheel—working, working, working, and still going nowhere—or were you recently on a tight deadline or working on a big project? Are you overwhelmed because you're trying to teach Suzy not to ask about your hair and do your job at the same time, or is it that your team is temporarily short-staffed? With projects or deadlines or personnel issues, there is usually (hopefully!) an end in sight. You can point to a date and say, "When I hand this in/launch this product/turn over this report, things will feel better." And even if you can't point to a specific project, timing is an important consideration. How long have you been feeling this way? We all have a bad week or couple of weeks from time to time. Burnout, on the other hand, can feel never ending, like that hamster on the wheel. It can feel like it's been going on forever and nothing you do will make it better or help it subside.

Another question—one that should be obvious, but we often forget to ask ourselves: Do you enjoy what you're doing? Even if you love your job, work is still work, and it will still wear on you from time to time. But if you feel engaged and invested, you're probably not suffering from burnout. Even if you're not particularly enjoying your work in this moment, it's worth digging a bit deeper. Do you get frustrated when you even think about going to work (burnout), or is it just that your work isn't stimulating? If the latter, it could be that you've outgrown your role and need to be challenged.

Burnout can result in a person being unreasonably short with colleagues, missing deadlines, and doing work that isn't up to their usual standards. It can cause you to be unmotivated and unfocused, or dissatisfied and uncaring when you do have an office success. But burnout can also manifest physically: it can lead to insomnia or, conversely, extreme fatigue. It can cause headaches or stomachaches or changes in appetite. If any of these symptoms are ongoing to the point of being chronic, then yes, you are likely burned out.

That said, only you can truly decipher if what you're experiencing is burnout or just regular work stress. Most of us have been swimming upstream for so long, expending double the energy just to stay in place, that we know the difference between feeling cynical or alone or disengaged because we are sick and tired of feeling sick and tired, and feeling run down because we've been putting in the work and the work is hard. During the phase of my career when I was doing double duty—working a full-time job while hustling to get ColorComm off the ground—I had a friend who used to always tell me I worked too much. "You're too hard on yourself!" she would say. "Your expectations are too high; that's why you're burned out." I was tired, sure, but I didn't think I was burned out. I had a fire in my belly. I was eager for success and I was willing to work for it. Still, I would find myself wondering if there was something to what she was saying. Should I slow down? Was this what being burned out feels like? Now I look back on those conversations and I think, *I wasn't putting too much pressure on myself; she wasn't putting enough pressure on herself! She didn't expect enough!* The truth is we all have different thresholds, and it's important to get in tune with our own capacity. If I had listened to my friend back then, I might have done less, which wouldn't have served my own goals.

I like working hard. I enjoy the rush of deadlines and having a full plate and feeling like I'm working toward something and have a purpose. There are times when my plate is less full and I feel like I'm coasting, and in those times my friends usually tell me I'm crazy. They'll point to this and that and say, "You're doing so much!" But only we can evaluate ourselves. My own burnout starts simmering when I am doing the same thing every day, when there is no challenge or excitement. For me, that's the kiss of death. For others, burnout is when their to-do list is too long because it feels insurmountable, and instead of feeling invigorated, they feel dread. Being able to identify your feelings and understand how to operate in professional environments can help you decipher if you're at risk of getting burned out, and if you already are.

Locate the Source

More often than not, burnout is a systemic problem rather than a personal one. A handful of companies are trying to institute policies that help relieve some of the extraneous demands that contribute to burnout. Organizations like Meta, Shopify, and Clorox have instituted "no-meeting days," because excessive and unproductive meetings—those hourlong gatherings that could have been an e-mail—have been identified as two major contributors to burnout (and they are general time-wasters). Bumble and LinkedIn each closed for a week in order to give employees a mental health break. For women of color, the most successful solutions will come when organizations or office places make changes that create more hospitable and equitable work environments. The truth is that burnout is probably easier to prevent than it is to fix. But that doesn't mean the only solution is to quit your job. It's one solution, for sure, but my hope is to help keep women of color *in* the workplace and to help them rise up, so my advice will never be to simply throw in the towel. Even if the problem is rooted in the culture of where you work, there will always be factors specific to you that compound the effects, which is why there might be two women of color at the same organization who have two different experiences. They have to deal with the same baseline workplace issues, but they are each dealing with their own contributing factors—factors that may have nothing to do with race or gender and that make their experience better or worse. If you can locate the source, or the cause, of your burnout, I do believe you can begin to relieve it.

There are reasons some people get more burned out than others. Part of that has to do with what's causing the burnout, and part of it has to do with how you cope with or manage the burnout when it starts to creep in. Let's start with the causes. Burnout can happen when you're too good at your job, but also when you're not good enough. It can be due to your own work habits or to factors dictated by your office. It would be nice to say that there's no such thing as being too good at your job, and in theory that's true. But as I mentioned in Chapter 6, when you're good at what you do and people know it, they will come to you with more work. The rock stars are always busy, because people know those people are consistent and reliable. If a manager or other leader needs something done quickly, he or she will go to the person they know can deliver. They will default to whoever won't need a ton of hand-holding or multiple rounds of revisions. And it's not just about work product—people will come to you for counsel or collaboration. They will pop over to your desk to discuss their projects or strategize for meetings. These are good problems to have—after all, you want to be the person that people go to and that they trust and respect. It's how you get in the meeting before the meeting. It's how you build relationships and get promotions. The danger, of course, is that when you're the go-to for everyone in the office, your plate will not only get full, it will start to overflow, and that can push a person to their limit.

This is where boundaries come in. As you know by now, I'm wary of workers invoking "boundaries" too soon. These days, plenty of employees enter an office place intent on establishing their boundaries before they've even done any work. But if you're the person everyone is continually counting on to take on that extra project or turn things around on a tight deadline, it's fair to start focusing on how to establish boundaries and how to enforce them. That doesn't mean you have to make a list of things you *don't* do. So often people cite boundaries when they say something like "I don't check e-mail after five." But hard-and-fast rules aren't the best way to get ahead—success relies on some level of flexibility and willingness to work with others. Still, you can manage expectations and be honest about what's on your plate. When someone asks you to take on a project, you should be able to say, "I'd love to help but I have six other high-priority things I'm doing right now, so I won't be able to get to this for at least a few weeks." And if your manager assigns you something where you don't have a choice but to do it right away, you can still communicate your workload. "In order to get this done in that time frame, I'll have to put something else on the back burner for a bit," you might say. Then, ask if they have a preference for which task you should set aside. Only you know the extent of your workload, so if you're in danger of burning out, be honest and do what you can to set boundaries so you can protect yourself and get ahead of it.

And then there is the opposite problem. Some people are simply not great at their jobs, and that can accelerate burnout as well. There's a business concept called the Peter Principle, which basically says that in organizations where there is a hierarchy (also known as a professional or corporate ladder), people will get promoted until they hit a point of incompetence. It makes sense if you think about it—you are good at your job, so you get a promotion. You're good at the next job, you get promoted again. In theory, this will keep happening until you step into a role where you don't excel, or you're not so good at your job, at which point you'll no longer get promoted. Obviously, it's not always so simple. As we well know, not everyone who deserves a promotion gets a promotion. But if you're someone who is struggling in a position, you're going to fast-track your burnout. You can get run-down simply from exerting the energy it takes to keep your head above water. If it takes you much more effort to get to the same place as the person next to you, it can be exhausting and also demoralizing. If your work is simply too difficult, you might feel frustrated and discouraged and generally negative about what's asked of you. And if your assignments take you an especially long time to complete, not only will it bleed into your personal life, knocking the work-life balance even more off-kilter, but your colleagues, if they don't know you're flailing, will just keep piling it on. It's enough to drive anyone to the brink—to the frustration and anger and disengagement that are the hallmarks of burnout.

A word of warning: it's tempting to stay quiet when you're in over your head. You don't want to call attention to yourself if you're struggling; I get it. But you aren't serving yourself or anyone around you by running yourself ragged, so it's important to communicate if you need help. And it's far better to do it sooner, before things have spiraled or work goes unfinished or you're at the end of your rope. People are receptive to requests for reinforcements if you make them with an appropriate cushion. When you leave others in a bind, that's when their understanding will be lacking.

Even if you're perfectly good at your job, it's possible that your work habits could use an overhaul and are crippling your ability to stave off burnout. So often, I've heard employees or colleagues complain about being overworked when the problem is less about their actual workload and more about their own ability to prioritize. If you're feeling the effects of burnout, ask yourself: Are you starting with a clear day? Are you blocking off chunks of time so that you can meet your deadlines? Are you coming into the office on time, or even a bit early, so you have a moment to breathe before the onslaught of e-mails or calls or texts begins? We put a lot of blame on our companies—and much of it is deserved—but we also need to take responsibility for our own contributions to burnout, because there are aspects that are within our control. Self-awareness in the office is hard, but it's incredibly important.

All these burnout factors are internally driven. A willingness to take on more than you can handle, an inability to ask for help, questionable work habits—it all starts with you and is, at least to a large extent, within your control. You've got to get your own house in order before you can start addressing the bigger ones. But there are definitely external factors that might be making things hard on you. Not just the systemic ones related to race or equity or general work culture. There are also situational factors. Being on a team that is poorly structured or short-staffed, having poor leadership or a lack of leadership altogether, having outgrown your role, or working with a colleague who is not carrying their own weight . . . all of this can add to your feelings of burnout. These are not all immediately resolvable, and you can't solve them on your own, but pinpointing the cause is the first step because then you have something specific to address with management or HR. You can cite specific issues that need to be addressed, and you're more likely to get solutions.

Ultimately, that's the goal: getting specific. It's why we always start with the question of "What do you need?" Because all work issues are easier to tackle when you can clearly identify the problem. "I'm feeling burned out; how do I fix it?" is a daunting question to answer. But "I'm feeling burned out because I take on too much work. I need to set boundaries so I don't have more than five projects on my plate at a time" is actionable. "Our team is burned out because we don't have proper guidance since our manager left; we need a leader in place" is something HR is more immediately equipped to help with. "I'm burned out because the requests are never-ending, and I need an uninterrupted chunk of time to get work done without constant interruptions" might help you realize that you need to come in earlier, or block that time off in your calendar. The more specific you can get with your need, the more specific you can get with your solution.

Preventative Medicine

Just as it's not the responsibility of women of color to fix race relations and inequities in the workplace, it's similarly not our responsibility to end burnout. In both cases, we are the ones who suffer the worst consequences—why should we also be the ones to come up with the solutions? That said, when it comes to burnout specifically, I do believe there are preventative measures that will save you a lot of pain. Considering that your top priority should be ensuring your own success, these steps are probably worth taking.

To start, take advantage of your paid vacation time. I am absolutely a proponent of working hard—in these post-pandemic times, people want to take it easier than they ever did before; if you are someone who wants to work hard, that will count for a lot—but the goal is not to burn yourself to the ground. Use your vacation days and your personal days in order to breathe, take some space away from the work, and allow yourself to think. I take vacations and I really use that time to clear my head and step away as much as possible. But also, I'm strategic about when I take that time. I do it based on my company's calendar. And yes, I understand that I'm the CEO, but you should take the same approach whether you are an entry-level employee or an executive leader. If you take a vacation in the weeks before a big project is due or leading up to your company's biggest event, you will not really be able to unplug. You will probably hear from the office, and it might make you think, *I knew it! This place can't even respect my time off!* If you're already burned out, and thus already cynical about your place of employment, it will be easy to chalk your disrupted vacation up to the horrors of your company. But timing matters. If you plan your time away strategically—during a quiet cycle or the offseason or after you hand in the project or whatever qualifies as a lull in the calendar at your company—you should be able to have a relatively quiet vacation (and if you can't, perhaps it really is time to reassess).

Taking care of your physical and mental health can also work wonders. Workouts can be a good outlet for stress (for me, that's a good long run; for you, it might be yoga); therapists can help you work through some of the emotional toll of work that eventually leads to burnout. The professional help that's been the most beneficial to me when I've needed to escape the burnout cycle is a career coach. There are a lot of misconceptions about what a career coach does. People are always surprised to hear I have one because of where I am in my professional life. "But you already know what you want to do!" they'll say. "You're doing it!" But a career coach's job isn't necessarily to help you decide what work you want to do. It's to help you navigate challenges in your chosen career and help you set goals and forge a path to success.

Setting goals is a way of taking ownership. Burnout can often result from feeling like you have no control over your career. It can feel really draining or even hopeless if you're constantly waiting for your job to happen *to* you— for a manager to come give you a promotion, or a recruiter to come offer you a new opportunity. Enter the career coach. This is a person who will help you find direction, because sometimes we're so caught up in the grind that we forget that we're actually working *toward* something. Career coaches will help you identify actionable steps that you can take to get closer to where you want to be. They will help you take the reins of your career, and that's really empowering. Career coaches can also help you define what success looks like to you—it might be more money, but it could also be flexibility, autonomy, an impressive title. Once you have a clear sense of where you want to go and how to get there, you will start to take on work or jobs that are stepping stones along that path.

So why do I have a career coach? Because even as the founder and CEO of my own company, a lot of days the work can feel like more of the same. Yes, much of the work we do at ColorComm is exciting and rewarding, and I am so happy to work for myself, but it's still work. A lot of it is a grind, and there's only a small team to help get it done, and like any hard worker there have been times when it felt like I was the one on the hamster wheel. My career coach prompted me to think through specific questions: What do I want to be doing day-to-day? Where do I want to take my company? Where do I see myself a year from now, and what are the things I am taking on now that will help me get there? When I was head-down in the work, I didn't take the time to think about those questions. My career coach helped me clarify my goals and specify a vision for the short term and the long term. She helped me identify the daily, weekly, and monthly steps I would need to take along the way. Let's say you have a goal to lose weight. You don't just wake up one day 20 pounds lighter. You need to think through how many calories you are going to cut, how much exercise you are going to do, how much more sleep you are going to get each day. It comes down to those individual pieces of the puzzle, and your career is no different. People who are presidents or CEOs of companies, they didn't wake up one day and get those titles bestowed upon them. They made purposeful choices throughout their careers. That approach is helpful whether your goal is to be in the C-Suite, to start your own company, or just to find yourself in a job that affords you flexibility and the ability to support yourself. You're not going to get where you want to be unless you are clear about your goals and plan accordingly, and if you need help with that, you can't look to mentors and sponsors. They don't get that granular. Mentors and sponsors are

15- or 30-minutes-once-a-month relationships. Career coaches can be as often as 90 minutes a week. It's an investment (yes, a career coach costs money, just like a gym or a therapist or a vacation costs money. Invest in yourself!), but what you get in return is a renewed sense of purpose in your career, and so much of burnout is characterized by a feeling of disconnection, or the sense that nothing you do really matters. It feels like you're running in place and nothing is going to change. Clarity around *why* you're doing the work you're doing, and *how* it will serve you in the end (and if it won't, how you can course-correct) can be a powerful antidote to a career plagued by burnout.

— 9 —

YOU NEED . . .
TO MOVE UP OR
MOVE OUT

In every job, there will come a time when you begin to wonder what's next. You've learned all you can in a position, or you're ready for more responsibility, a better title, or more money. These days, it can feel like the quickest way to climb the ladder is to jump from one job to the next, but there's a tricky dance to career advancement. Hopping around and amassing as many organizations on your résumé as possible is not a career, it's just a collection of jobs. A career is a journey, a logical progression of roles in service of a greater professional purpose. And like most journeys, it takes time. Careers span decades—many of us will be working for 30, 40, even 50 years—so it's foolish to think you should be shooting up the ladder in a matter of months. Your professional life is a marathon of doing the work and learning new lessons along the way. Acquiring skills, producing wins, getting feedback, learning to solve problems, correcting mistakes, building relationships—all of these are critical steps, and they can't be rushed.

That said, as you conquer work challenges and create your professional tool kit, the intention is that you will start taking on new opportunities and continue to strive toward your greater goal. That could look like a promotion, or taking on a new position at a different company in your industry, or switching industries entirely, or starting to work for yourself. The key is to not get stuck in a position where you feel stagnant. We already know that stagnation can lead to burnout, but also you won't feel fulfilled in your career unless you believe you are moving toward something. Forward momentum looks different for everyone—you might take a pay cut in order to work at your dream company, or make a lateral move because you want to switch industries—which is why being clear on your career goals and having your own strategic plan is so critical. (You can do this with a career coach, but you can also do it on your own—think about where you want to be in one, five, ten years, and then outline the skills you'll need and the specific steps it might take to get there.) It can be tricky to navigate professional timing. How do you know when it's time to pursue a move up, and how do you know when it's time to move on? How long is too long to stay in one place, and when should you ask for the promotion or the raise? You don't want to stay somewhere so long that you get stuck, but your résumé should speak to your ability to execute. Women of color often wait until they are burned out or frustrated before the question of next steps become top of mind, and by then it's usually too late to make progress at a pace that will feel satisfying (when you hit that wall you usually want to leave, and leave now). We're so busy trying to perform, trying to keep our heads down, trying to ignore daily microaggressions, that we forget to step outside ourselves and think big picture. Like I said, it's a tricky dance, and as with most dances, timing is everything.

The Case for Staying Put

In today's world, the default approach to moving up the ladder is to look for a new job. Applying to an outside organization can feel much less daunting than having a seemingly difficult conversation in which you request a raise or a promotion. But I want to challenge anyone who feels that way to reframe their thinking. When times at work get tough, ask yourself what do you need in order to be happy where you are rather than jump ship. There are a lot of benefits to staying in place, at least for a stretch. First, the obvious: a lot of companies incentivize employees to stay longer. They might offer stock options or a vesting schedule that favors longevity. They might increase the number of paid days off the longer you stick around. There's also the fact that it takes a long time to get in the door at most companies. Interviewing for a job is not a speedy endeavor. Once you've jumped through all the hoops and landed the position, you owe it to yourself (and perhaps to your employer) to give it your all. I've heard too many people decide it's time to leave a job when they've barely even started because it wasn't what they expected, or they have impostor syndrome, or it's not the perfect fit. But just because a position isn't your ultimate dream job, or you got feedback you didn't like, that's not a reason to up and leave. You will run into challenges no matter where you go. Jobs are called *work* for a reason. The more you can practice navigating difficult situations and becoming solution oriented, the better off you will be when the next opportunity does come along.

In any career, the hope is that you are always learning, but the truth is, in the first year of a job, it's hard to
learn much other than the very specific requirements of
your position. Year one is all about getting up to speed on
your role and your company. You may learn how to use
your organization's unique systems or how to execute your
particular function, but you aren't likely to acquire the
professional skills that will prepare you for moving to the
next level. In order to learn those things, you need time
to get feedback and incorporate it, and improve and grow.
You need time to see what works and what doesn't. You
need time to actually *do* things that can create change at
your company or with your clients. You also aren't likely,
in only one year, to develop the trust and relationships
that are required to really thrive and feel satisfied in any
given role. In any job, and at any rung of the professional
ladder, people desire autonomy. They want to be trusted
so that it doesn't feel like their boss is hounding them all
the time or like they are being micromanaged. They want
to be free to get their work done in their own way, so long
as they deliver what their managers or clients need when
they need it. People are happier in roles where they can
take a doctor's appointment during the day or pick their
kids up early without being questioned. But that kind of
freedom needs to be earned. It comes as a result of performance, of demonstrating reliability, of being a team
player. It comes as a result of time.

Pushing through hard times at your job rather than
leaving the moment you hit the one-year mark will serve
you in all these ways, but let us not underestimate, also,
how good that commitment will look on your résumé
when you *do* finally decide it's time to apply elsewhere.
Every industry is different, but in general, a résumé that
shows a new job every year is a concern from an HR

standpoint. It indicates that you're a hopper, that maybe you don't know what you're doing, or that it may not be worth it for this company to invest in you because you'll leave the second the next shiny opportunity comes along. If a company hires you, they want you to stick around long enough to meaningfully contribute. If you are going to swoop in, possibly influence the culture and the people, and just as quickly head out, it will be best not to hire you at all. Taking a new job every year might also indicate to anyone paying attention that you are more interested in your own brand than you are in doing the work. And listen, I'm all about prioritizing your own success. That's what this book is about. But you will have an easier time creating opportunities for yourself if you demonstrate your ability to commit and contribute. Opportunities come to those who are killing it, and the résumé of a person who can't hold on to a job for longer than 12 months doesn't exactly give that impression.

As you ascend to more leadership-level positions, even a new job every two years is a bit suspect. I would suggest committing (not verbally, but to yourself) to two or three years minimum once you've accepted a new position. Obviously, if you're in a toxic work environment or you're truly miserable, that's a different story—people are entitled to the occasional blip on the résumé. But in general, two to three years shows that you stayed long enough to have a meaningful impact on your workplace. Three to five years shows that you value security, stability, growth. More than five shows dedication. It shows mutual respect between you and the company that employed you, and it shows you are someone who can keep long-term commitments.

Asking for More

Just because you stay at the same place for three or four years doesn't mean you should stay at the same pay level or in the same position for that entire stretch. The hope is that when you show loyalty to a company, they will show loyalty in return by working to retain you and rewarding your hard work with new titles or increased compensation. As we already know, the data around women of color and promotions or raises is bleak. We get promotions at a far lower rate than men, and at a lower rate than white women. Same goes for raises. What that means is that we need to come to the discussion even more prepared, and we need to be ready for an ongoing conversation rather than a quick ask.

It's not always easy to know when it's time to ask for a raise. There's a commonly held belief that once you've been at a company for a year, it's time to demand more money. But that's a pretty arbitrary rule, and if you're sitting around waiting for your company to say, *Well, you've been here a year/two years/three years, time for more money*, well, you're probably going to be waiting for a long time. Simply having been at a job for a certain amount of time is not enough to warrant a raise anymore. So when *is* it time? I know that "it depends" is an annoying answer, but it really does. Situational factors will affect whether you're likely to be met with the resounding yes you're looking for, and they include your work performance, the company's overall performance, the time of year you are asking (in relation to the fiscal year), your company's promotion schedule, and more. But there are no hard-and-fast rules. If your work product is indispensable, you could get a promotion or raise off cycle if your company thinks you're a flight risk. Some questions to consider as you decide if now is the right time to start the conversation: What goals did your manager outline for you when you first started? Have you reached them? What has the feedback been about your performance? Can you do your job in your sleep? If you haven't reached your goals, if your feedback is still lukewarm, if your job is still challenging, then don't waste your time asking for more money yet, even if you've been on the job for a year or longer. You haven't earned it, and asking for a pay increase will only give the impression that you don't have a realistic sense of how far you've come or how far you have left to go. You don't want your manager to think you have no perspective on your own performance.

I once had two employees, at two different levels of the organization, come to me at the same time—not literally, but it was during the same week, which pretty much felt simultaneous—both asking for a raise. I could tell they had collaborated and strategized their asks together and I have to admit, I did not appreciate the way it was approached. I don't fault them for asking for more—we should all be asking for more! Women of color deserve more than we are getting. I'm confident we all agree on that. But these women clearly hadn't done the self-reflection necessary to establish whether they actually *deserved* a raise. It was almost as if they had been talking over drinks and gotten themselves worked up about deserving more and set a plan in motion to tag-team me. They knew the company was hiring for a couple of new roles, so they were trying to get more money before that cash was earmarked for another individual. Smart thinking, maybe, but each of them used the same flimsy argument for why they deserved more: "We are loyal; we are working hard." Unfortunately, that's not a good enough reason to warrant a pay bump. Neither employee had been in their position long enough to demonstrate marked improvement from when they were hired or from when they'd gotten their last raise. In fact, one of the women had gotten a raise pretty recently. They'd both had a few weeks of working extra hard because our entire company had a lot going on, but their output wasn't consistent, and I was put off by the fact that they asked for more money because they thought more money was available, not because they had earned it. If you're approaching your manager asking for a raise, you need to be ready to show you have been adding value beyond just handing in your work on time. How hard you're working isn't the barometer—after all, you might be working really hard because the work is harder for you than it is for your colleagues. It may take you longer to get it done. Are you increasing the bottom line? Are you bringing in new clients? Are you helping to retain customers? Are you helping other employees get up to speed faster? Are you the go-to for senior leaders when they need a team player at your level? If you can take a holistic, 360-degree approach to demonstrate how you are helping to move the needle on business objectives, then you've got the case for more money because it would be a challenge for the business if you left.

When it comes to promotions specifically (versus just asking for a raise), it's important to consider what work you're already doing. Ideally, before you even request a promotion, you've already tackled some of the work that will be required of the next level. That way, you'll have a taste of what the next role requires, and you can use your success with that work as evidence that you're ready for the next step. If you haven't taken on any of those additional responsibilities yet; if you're not raising your hand for those assignments or having them funneled to you, your boss will probably want that to happen before they officially move you into the position.

Another aspect of getting a promotion is leadership. Are you volunteering to take point on new projects? Are you mentoring or managing others, even if only in an informal capacity? You need to show initiative and agency if you want to move up.

Let's say you've done everything right; you've checked off all the things I've outlined already, and you are completely confident that you deserve a promotion, or at the very least more money. Even in these circumstances, you have to go into the conversation with your manager with the understanding that the discussion will be ongoing. Ideally, you've been having regular touch-bases with your boss and you've discussed shared goals, so you both know that you're working toward the next step and it won't be a total surprise when you make the ask. But don't expect to ask for more money and to see a bigger paycheck the following week—anticipate that it will take three to six months from when you first inquire. I know, it sounds like a long time, but that's why it's so important to not wait until you're burned out or overworked to start the conversation. First of all, some companies only dole out raises at certain times of the year. Some managers use the first raise request—even for a rock-star employee—as an opportunity to establish a new set of goals that, when accomplished, will trigger the bump. Some managers may agree you deserve a raise but need to send it through multiple levels of approvals, or they may need to put in for the budget increase. In bigger corporations, raises often happen from April to June. During the second quarter people get promoted in bulk because by then a company has a sense of how their year is going to look financially and who they can afford to move up. These on-cycle promotions usually come in a percentage of your salary—it's a formula, and the percentage is usually relatively small because it's being doled out across a large group of people. If you are someone who is truly excelling—that is, if you left the job your company would be kicking themselves—you might want to shoot for an off-cycle promotion, because there's freedom to ask for more if you aren't beholden to a specific percentage that's going to everyone.

Speaking of asking for more, it's critical that if you are asking for a raise, you have a number in mind. Don't wait for your boss to make an offer. You are the one doing the asking, so it's incumbent upon you to start the negotiation. Be ready to say, "I am looking for this amount more, I'm looking for this title, and these are the reasons why I think I deserve it." I once had an employee ask me for a raise and when I asked her how much she had in mind she basically just said, "I don't know; I just think I deserve a raise." Well, um, okay. "What does that mean?" I said. "You want me to tell you what raise you should get?" If you don't go in with a specific ask, you will get lowballed. So come with a number that meets your value but is also aligned with what your company usually grants. Don't come in asking for something completely unrealistic, because it sets a bad tone and makes it impossible for your manager to say yes, even when they want to.

Taking Your Talents Elsewhere

While I'm an advocate for digging in your heels and at least trying to get ahead in your current place of work, sometimes it's clear that the only way you are going to progress in your career is to get a new job in a new company. That might be because you want to try working in a different industry, or because there really are no avenues for advancing at your organization. Maybe someone was recently hired for the position that would be your next step, so you know there won't be an opening anytime soon. Maybe there's a company where you've always wanted to work, and the perfect role just opened up. Maybe you want to try something totally new, and that job doesn't exist where you currently work. These are all perfectly legitimate reasons to start looking for a new job.

It might also become clear to you that despite your attempts to advance internally, you're never going to get the promotion or the raise that you deserve. It's important to pay attention to this, because you don't want to spin your wheels in a role with no future. Unless your manager is firing you or laying you off, they are not going to reveal that you have no opportunities for advancement. They may know that you will never get the promotion you're asking for, but they're not going to tell you that! They will dangle things in front of you, promising a promotion "down the line" or "soon" or "eventually," in hopes that they will get as much as they can from you without having to invest much in you. And they will do this for as long as you let them. So, what are the signs that the promised raise or promotion is never coming? How can you tell that the only way you'll be able to take your next career step is if you leave? To start, if people are getting promoted around you as you stay in one place, that's a clue. If people who started at the same time as you, or after you, are consistently climbing the ladder while you are told to be patient, well, don't bother being patient. The thing you are waiting for is likely never coming. If you are getting shut out of decision-making moments and meetings, if you are being regularly passed over for new opportunities, if everything you've been promised—whether it's a promotion or a raise or the chance to take on new work or attend a conference—keeps getting delayed, then your company is not priming you for growth. If there is consistent noninvestment, then it's absolutely time to find a place that *will* invest in you.

There might also be instances when you just really don't like your job. It could be the people, the office culture, your boss. If you are miserable every day—not just bored, but truly unhappy—it's probably not worth sticking it out. There will be other jobs with more pleasant environments. I had one job on Capitol Hill that was great in a lot of ways—I learned important skills, I made important connections—but there were some colleagues with whom I just did not jell. There was some nastiness and preferential treatment of my colleagues that made my experience incredibly unpleasant. Toxic work environments are real, and I left that job not only because I was miserable, but also because all signs pointed to the fact that I was on the chopping block. There was a consistency of behavior that told me I wasn't welcome, and at the end of the day, the goal is to have an enjoyable experience where you work. Every day isn't going to feel like a party, but we all know the difference between a bad day or two and overarching misery.

Once you've decided to apply for other jobs, start by going through all the regular channels, like LinkedIn or any of the job sites that are specific to your industry. You should also reach out to those contacts at other companies that you've spent all that time nurturing relationships with. Ask for discretion, since you don't need anyone at your current job knowing you're looking, but let your contacts know that you're exploring opportunities and ask them to keep you in mind. And finally, keep your ear to the ground. Pay attention to anything you hear about who is coming and going in your industry, because if one person leaves, another person has to replace them, and maybe that person should be you. That's exactly how I got that job on Capitol Hill in the first place. I knew that the communications director in that office had recently been hired by my firm, so I kept my eyes peeled for the job-opening and reached out as soon as it was posted. When it comes to finding new gigs, my best advice is to keep your ear to the ground and your relationships hot.

Layoffs Are Coming

Layoffs happen. Some companies do rounds of layoffs routinely to trim the fat, so to speak. Some organizations cut entire divisions or go through internal restructures that eliminate positions. Budget cuts—due to a company's struggles or the greater economic climate—might require letting go of lesser performers. Some companies go under entirely, putting the full employee roster out of work. Getting laid off is not necessarily a judgment on your individual performance, but it can certainly feel personal if you are told unexpectedly that you no longer have a paycheck. It also feels personal if you are a woman of color, one of only a few at a company, and the majority of the folks who were laid off look like you. Research shows that women and employees of color are deemed "redundant" or "nonessential" more often than their white male colleagues.[1] We are the first on the chopping block when layoffs loom. During the pandemic, the outlook was even worse—women of color were the hardest hit by layoffs and job loss.[2] Understanding how to see a potential layoff coming, and how to bounce back afterward, is a vital aspect of continuing along your career path, even in the face of hardship.

The biggest indicator that a layoff could be coming for you is workflow. If your workload is light and has been consistently for a long (or even long*ish*) period of time, that's not a great sign. If everyone or most of the people on your team have a light load, it might mean there's just not enough work to justify your position, or that rather than three people at your level on your team, there's only enough work for two. On the other hand, you might suddenly notice that your workload is light even though the colleagues around you keep getting more and more assignments piled on. If your workflow seems to have dried up even though you keep asking for more, take note. If people seem unwilling to talk about future plans with you, take note of that, too. When I was laid off in my first job, I had been asking my manager questions about my future, and she kept asking me to "hold off for now." It struck me as strange at the time, and I should have known it was a sign, but no one had taught me that, so I figured the best thing to do was to sit back and be patient. I worried that maybe I was being too pushy. But it's not pushy to want to move forward! Being proactive is generally looked upon favorably. If your managers seem to be getting frustrated with your ambition rather than encouraging it, there's usually something bigger at play.

Relationships are another critical piece when it comes to anticipating layoffs. When cuts are coming, *someone* usually knows. Word gets around. The more allies you have within your company, the more likely you are to catch wind of the company's plans. Of course, these relationships could also be what saves you from getting cut altogether. Having powerful people in your corner could be the difference maker, because those people can vouch for you when decisions are being made and names of "dispensable" employees are getting thrown into the ring. If you run point on a number of important clients, or are the person who attracts them, those relationships could also keep you safe. Similarly, if your colleagues have relationships that will obviously keep them safe, you could be at risk by default. If one of your colleagues is the niece of someone in the C-Suite or the son of an important client, they are probably not getting the boot. Your company is not going to lay off a celebrity daughter, even if her output isn't stellar. Sometimes, that leaves you in the hot seat.

You might also notice, one day, that your company is gathering information from you on processes or procedures. *Remind me of the process for working with this vendor? Can you walk me through the stages involved in producing that annual report?* If this comes out of nowhere, or from a higher-up who usually wouldn't concern himself with that level of detail, it could be a clue that they're coming for you. Companies don't want to cut anyone loose until they've gathered all the information necessary to train the next person.

Unfortunately, knowing how to spot a layoff usually isn't enough to save yourself. By the time you can see it coming down the pike, it's usually too late to course-correct. Layoffs happen fast. Companies don't plan to lay someone off and then wait six months to deal with it. If business needs require cutting people from the payroll, an organization will act fast in order to get back on track. You likely won't have a window to improve your performance and convince them to change their minds, which is why establishing yourself from the outset is so important. At the end of the day, when choosing who to cut, a company looks at performance, likeability, and connection, and none of these can be turned around overnight.

Let's say you anticipate getting laid off, and you don't think there's anything you can do about it. You're still better off knowing ahead of time. If you've got a sense that you might be on the chopping block, then you need to start developing a plan. First of all, you want to gather all you can from your company before your access is cut off. Make sure you have all your contacts saved somewhere other than in your work e-mail. Maybe you want to reach out to HR and ask them what to expect. Your questions can be simple: Do you anticipate layoffs this quarter? If so, will packages be issued to employees? If you're laid off with a decent severance package, then you'll be much better off than if you're cut with no safety net. If that information is available ahead of time, all the better. You'll also, of course, want to start saving. Even if there *is* a package, you never know how long it will take you to land the next job. If you believe your paycheck is in jeopardy, you might want to halt your spending for a bit, or at least cut back.

You also want to leave your company with a strong portfolio of your work product. If you think any jobs in the company are in danger, start getting together documentation and examples of your output. Try to gather any internal data that will demonstrate the success of your projects. Even if you think you'll be safe, it's smart to be ready—employees often overestimate their own security, and the moment you're let go you could lose access to documents and work that you wish you had saved. The intention is to do whatever is necessary before you're laid off to ensure you're a good candidate for the next job you want. That might entail reaching out to your contacts and asking for introductions. Keep in mind, you want to leave on good terms with as many people as possible. Industries are small. You don't know who knows who, or who you might work with again. It might be tempting to try to burn it all down in your wake, especially if you feel mistreated, but don't take the bait. Looking out for yourself means

WHAT DO YOU NEED?

parting ways with as much dignity as possible because it will behoove you down the line. If layoffs are coming, your entire focus should turn to how to set yourself up for success.

On to the Next

When I was laid off from my very first job, I was embarrassed and ashamed. I lived with my aunt in Maryland at the time, and I was commuting 90 minutes into Washington, D.C., every day. It was 30 minutes from my aunt's house to the train station, then I had to take two different trains—the whole experience was awful. The only perk of getting laid off, in theory, was that I could get three hours of my time back each day. Instead, I was too embarrassed to tell my family, so I still got up early every day and commuted into D.C. I would leave the house at 7 A.M. each morning and head to the Georgetown library, where I spent the day applying for jobs. Each day, I called specific companies to ask for the e-mail addresses of their HR people so I could e-mail the hiring managers directly. I would send full application packages in the mail. I tried everything I could think of to be creative and stand out in a crowded market, and I did that for a month and a half! Every day, commuting for an hour and a half both ways. I applied to hundreds of jobs a week and got three interviews, one of which eventually turned into an offer. In less than two months, I had a new job, though I felt like it took forever at the time.

As I look back on that experience, there are certainly things I wish I could tell my younger self. First of all, there is no reason to feel ashamed if you get laid off. It happens more often than you might think, and most of the world's most successful people have been laid off or fired at some point. You're in good company. I would also probably tell young Lauren to save her gas money! I could have gone around the corner to the coffee shop and gotten just as much done. But at the time I needed to be in that library environment—I wanted to be surrounded by focused and driven people. Your environment really can play into your focus, your thought process, and ultimately your success. But aside from those two notes, there are so many things I did in the aftermath of that layoff that I would do again, and that I would suggest to anyone else in the same circumstance. If you are laid off, don't take an extended break in order to feel sorry for yourself or wallow or even enjoy the supposed benefits of unemployment. No. Start looking for the next opportunity right away. It's like working out. A body in motion stays in motion. The more time you take off—because you're hurt or offended or because you have decided that now you're going to wait to find the absolutely perfect job—the further away you get from the skills, the corporate speak, and the regular motions of how jobs work. The more time you take away, the farther you move yourself from the knowledge that you need for the next opportunity. For me, it took going to the library and treating looking for a job like a full-time job to land the next gig. There was no watching TV and eating snacks; I put all my energy and effort into staying in the game. After all, I was paying rent to live with my aunt. I needed an income. I didn't have the luxury of being financially supported by someone, I had no cushion to support time off. In retrospect, I think that helped add fuel to my fire—I was driven to get another job because I needed the income to live!—but whether or not that's your circumstance, you should act like it is. Go after the next job with gusto.

And finally, as for what to say to the HR rep or hiring manager about why you left your last position? While being laid off is nothing to be ashamed of, you don't necessarily need to lead with it. You can absolutely just say that you are looking for new opportunities, and that you want to build new skills. But sometimes a company will have such mass layoffs that everyone in the industry knows about it. That could actually work to your advantage because people want to help—this happened at Twitter after Elon Musk took over. If nearly half of a company's employees are cut, hiring managers at other places know it's not a commentary on performance. But if you're sensitive about it, you certainly don't need to shout it from the rooftops. Still, if you're asked directly, you have to be honest. Instead of saying, "I was laid off," you could say, "My team/position was eliminated," or "There was a reorg"—people understand the implications, but it points less to your performance and more to business needs.

Careers are about progress. Whether you move up somewhere or apply elsewhere, whether you leave on your own accord or you're pushed out, every change is an opportunity to grow and move in the direction of where you eventually hope to be. It's an opportunity to flex all the muscles we've covered in this book, because if you are going to get ahead, you'll have to rely on your ability to know if you belong, build and activate relationships, signal value, do the work, and take risks. The game is always being played—your job is to work it to your advantage.

PART FOUR

Becoming an Ally

— 10 —

YOU NEED . . .
TO UNDERSTAND SOMEONE
ELSE'S PERSPECTIVE
(AND WHY IT MATTERS FOR YOU)

This book is for women of color. I hope it has felt like an honest, inside look at the professional game that is always being played around us, the one that we have long been shut out of. I want women of color to successfully navigate the workforce as it currently exists, because if we sit back and wait for systems to change, we could be waiting forever. But let me be clear: The systems DO need to change. Some of that change is going to require women of color getting into leadership positions so they can lead by example and create change from within. But if major systematic changes are going to happen, our white colleagues are going to have to do some of the heavy lifting. It's the leaders in any organization who have the most power to create change or overhaul the culture. And while it's become increasingly common for white employees to call themselves allies, the action isn't always there to back it up. Oftentimes, that's a function of white employees simply not knowing what good allyship looks like. Sure, sometimes white professionals truly don't care—they say they're allies because it sounds good, but as long as they're getting ahead, inclusion doesn't actually matter to them. But I believe that many of those who say they are allies really do want to do the right thing. The final section of this book, this chapter and the next, is for those readers—the white workers, largely white women, who want to create change but don't know how. (Research shows that white women are more likely than white men to identify as allies or to take allyship actions.) These workers don't know what to do to make the work experience better for their colleagues of color, and they often don't even know how to explain to their other white colleagues *why* increasing equity will benefit the whole. Because let me be clear: equity and inclusion are not just about people being kinder to each other or increasing diversity for the sake of increasing diversity. Equity and inclusion will increase a company's bottom line. They will result in more productive workers. They will create thriving workplaces. These two chapters are for the white readers who truly want to walk the walk: they will help you understand *why* you (and your company) will benefit from a more equitable environment and, more important, *how* you can begin to create it.

All Together Now

Workplaces—regardless of the cultural or racial breakdown of their employees—are comprised of a hodgepodge of people with different life experiences and perspectives, many of whom don't understand each other or see eye to eye. People come from different backgrounds, different education levels, different parts of the country. Some come from two-parent homes, others don't; some have siblings, others have none. Some went to Ivy League schools, others to state schools, and some to community college while others didn't go to college at all. All of these differences are important, because most businesses want to reach groups or consumers beyond just one religion or political affiliation or sexual orientation. The organizations behind products or services want to appeal to a wide expanse of people, so they need a similarly wide expanse of employees who can understand and communicate with the consumers who contribute to their bottom line.

This, of course, is one reason why inclusion is so important. Representation matters. Not only is it hard to message a group of people you can't relate to or don't understand, it's also incredibly easy to get it wrong even when you try. There are countless examples of companies that have released offensive products or campaigns that have made entire groups of people scratch their heads and say, "What were they thinking?" Pepsi's 2017 ad where Kendall Jenner seemingly drops into a protest with her can of soda and single-handedly stops police brutality, is one example. Or Gucci's 2019 turtleneck sweater that seemed to mimic blackface. These egregious mistakes leave companies scrambling to cover their tracks and issue apologies, and they bring momentary attention to the diversity, or lack thereof, in an organization's workforce. Crises too often are the first time companies or the public think about issues of inclusion—and of course by then the company has waited too long.

But diversity alone isn't what's most important. Just having people from other groups in the room isn't enough if those people are not included, not given a voice, not given decision-making power. If someone of color was in the room when the Gucci or Pepsi campaigns were created, but that person was the *only* person of color, would they have spoken up? And if they had, would they have been heard? Just as important as hiring diverse employees is *including* them. It's critical to foster strong relationships between employees who may not look alike or who have different backgrounds, because the diversity only matters if everyone has a voice, if everyone actually listens to one another and asks one another's opinions. It only counts for something if the diverse group of employees can work together in ways that are efficient and productive.

Calling on any collection of individuals to work together, day in and day out, to produce great output is a big ask. No matter if the differences are racial, geographic, socioeconomic, political, or just which sports team you root for, the fact that colleagues can co-exist at all—let alone collaborate and be productive!—is pretty miraculous. And yet, it's so important. Interpersonal conflicts can have detrimental effects on a company's bottom line. People in conflict (even it's an unspoken or passive-aggressive conflict rather than a confrontational one) dedicate time to the conflict that they could be spending on producing quality work. Instead of focusing on finishing a project, they stew about how they were mistreated. Instead of coming together with a colleague to brainstorm the next great idea, they come together to complain about their *other* colleague who said something offensive, or about their boss, who once again asked about their hair.

When there are friction points within departments or teams, the work product is affected. People who feel disrespected by a company don't invest their best effort into that company. If someone has been demeaned by someone on their team, whether on purpose or by accident, they won't be anxious to jump into another project with that person. Time lines will get delayed, deadlines will be missed. Projects that were supposed to be collaborative turn into solo efforts. Resentments between colleagues translate into inefficient teams, and when employees need to spend energy just to get comfortable in an unwelcoming environment, they will have less energy to give to the work tasks required of them. Even if there isn't a specific conflict, if employees don't feel comfortable with one another, their collaboration will be stilted. Perhaps they'll be so focused on saying the right thing, or on *not* saying the wrong thing, that they won't be able to get into the flow of producing good work. Simply put, teams that get along and work well together perform better. Everything that takes away from doing the work is a distraction, and distractions are harmful to the bottom line. All of which is to say, connecting with your colleagues of color shouldn't only be important because you want to be a better person, it's important because it will improve your business.

I want to point out that connecting with another person doesn't necessarily make you an ally. Allyship requires sustained action, and not everyone is built for it. And that's okay! I'll get more into what makes a true ally in a bit, but for now, know this: even if you're not cut out for full-fledged allyship, you can still be a good colleague. It starts there. Even if you can't commit to prolonged action, you can at the very least get to know, and try to connect with, the people you work with, especially those with whom you may not, on the surface, have anything in common. This is the first step toward seeing them as humans rather than numbers. And if this sounds like a tall order, if it feels like you'll never relate to a particular person, remember that you both chose to work at the same organization. You have that in common. Even if you come from different backgrounds and have different perspectives on most things, you accepted a job at the same workplace, which means you likely believe in a common vision, a common mission, and common values. If nothing else, you are aligned on that, and you should be able to use that as a point of connection.

One thing I hear so often from our ColorComm members is that they have to work really hard in majority-white environments to get to know the people they work with, and usually they are the only ones putting in the effort. These are employees who are already working hard just to exist as the "only" or one of the few, not to mention doing the work required of their job, but then they have to do the extra homework of figuring out how to infiltrate and connect with the majority culture. On the other hand, the white employees, because they can so easily connect with the people who look like them, don't spend nearly the same amount of time learning about the people of color they work with. But remember, if you want to increase and improve the output of your team, the connection should be a two-way street. When the effort is entirely one-sided, resentment ensues.

If you are someone who grew up surrounded by very little diversity—or maybe you've had diversity around you, but everyone's always kept to themselves, the Black kids with the Black kids, the Asian kids with the Asian kids, the white kids with the white kids, and so on—challenges can arise from simply not knowing how to connect. You may not have had the opportunity or the benefit of being surrounded by intelligent people who are at your level but don't look like you. You might have a heightened concern about saying the wrong thing. This is why it's important to not just have diversity within a company, but also DEI education and training for employees. Of course, it can take years of education and real-life experience to change views or beliefs that were formed during childhood. You aren't suddenly going to be trained in all things DEI after one session. But the more you are taught about the intricacies of how to connect or what not to say—the more education you get surrounding all those concerns you might currently be navigating blind, or not navigating at all because you don't feel equipped—the better chance you'll have of working with your colleagues in ways that will serve your company, and ultimately serve you. Because it's your work product that will benefit, and your performance that will improve.

Getting to Know Each Other

When it comes to diversity in the workplace, the business case is pretty cut-and-dried. Research shows that diverse companies have 2.5 times higher cash flow per employee[1] and are 70 percent more likely to capture new markets.[2] Diverse management teams see an average increase in revenue of 19 percent.[3] Diverse teams are 35 percent more likely to outperform their industry's average financial returns. Studies show diverse teams are more productive decision-makers, better innovators, and faster problem-solvers. When diverse teams are working well together, they will pretty much always lead to more success. When they aren't . . . well, as I said, success can get derailed pretty quickly.

This book is not a DEI manual. It can't take the place of proper training. But I've talked enough in this book about microaggressions and the offenses that women of color have to regularly suffer in the workplace that I want to be sure that those of you who are reading this understand what I'm referring to and how to avoid being the offenders. Psychologist Kevin Nadal, an expert and author who writes about microaggressions and their effects, defines microaggressions as "everyday, subtle, intentional—and oftentimes unintentional—interactions or behaviors that communicate some sort of bias." They aren't necessarily overtly racist, and the person committing them may not even know they are being offensive, but they still have the effect of making the person on the receiving end feel othered. When people tell me I am "articulate for a Black girl," that is a microaggression. So is asking an Asian colleague where she is "really from." Commenting on someone's name, asking about a Black woman's hair, asking why your Muslim colleague wears a hijab—these are all microaggressions. Such comments often take the form of supposed compliments or observations or questions because the asker is "just curious." It usually calls specific attention to something that makes a person different from the majority, and it makes that person feel that they are on the outside. Of course, everyone is different, but microaggressions say that this person's differences aren't "normal."

Don't be fooled by the word *micro* in *microaggression*. The *micro* refers to the fact that the dig is subtle rather than overt, but it doesn't mean the effect on the recipient is minor. Consistently landing on the receiving end of slights that you are just supposed to smile at and accept because someone "didn't mean to be racist" is exhausting. Microaggressions have been shown to lead to increased stress, isolation, and depression. When discussing microaggressions, people commonly use the expression "death by a thousand cuts," because honestly, that's what it can feel like: small, repeated digs that chip away at your morale on a job. Research has even shown that being continually subjected to microaggressions can lead to physical ailments like thyroid problems or high blood pressure. According to the McKinsey & Company and LeanIn.Org 2021 *Women in the Workplace* report, "women who regularly experience microaggressions are twice as likely as those who don't to be burned out, more than twice as likely to report feeling negatively about their job, and almost three times as likely to say they've struggled to concentrate at work in the past few months due to stress."[4] It's a real problem.

Microaggressions are also especially taxing because they can be extremely hard to confront someone about. If a white colleague commits a microaggression and they don't know they did it, calling them out can result in some extreme defensiveness. No one responds well to being told they did something racist, especially if they truly believe their intentions were the opposite. I hope that if your colleague of color tells you that you've done something offensive, you'll believe it and try to change, but it doesn't always unfold that way. And oftentimes the offended party doesn't even want to confront the offender to discuss the problem. Instead—and especially if it has happened repeatedly— they retract, they distance themselves, they get mad. They might give a lesser effort and make the offender carry the load. They might be slow to respond to e-mails or even ask to get transferred. They might quiet quit. There are business tactics people take when they are offended, consciously or not, and these tactics stall productivity.

So how can you do the work to get to know your colleagues of color without asking questions or making comments that might inadvertently offend? Start by getting to know the *person*. Why did she choose to work at this company? What are her professional goals? What is her favorite TV show? What are her hobbies? You don't have to make an observation about her name, her style of dress, or her hair. These observations don't actually teach you anything about the person you are trying to learn about. If you have a question you aren't sure about, if you're curious about something and think it's okay to ask because you "want to learn," stop and ask yourself some questions before you speak. Why do you have this question? Does the answer actually matter to your work product? Will it help increase collaboration? If you only ask yourself one question, ask yourself this: Is this thing that I'm curious about something that will help me and my colleague work together? If whatever you're about to ask is offensive, then the answer will almost certainly be no. *You* might feel better, because your curiosity is assuaged, but they will feel worse. In general, try to focus your questions on business and work and less on the superficial topics like how a person sounds or looks. And if your curiosity is burning so hot that you simply cannot focus until you get your questions answered, might I remind you of the Internet? Google. Almost any question you have, the answer is online. It's not a foolproof option. The Internet isn't always a reliable source, but please do not burden your colleagues with your curiosities. Find a different approach.

And while we're on the subject of questions, please, for the love of God, if you aren't clear on your colleague of color's name, ask for clarification. But ask early! On the first day, when you meet your new colleague, don't be scared to say, "Can you repeat that for me, please? I want to be sure I get it right." In the moment, you might not have heard it correctly. Or maybe it really is a name you haven't heard before. This is fine. People appreciate someone caring enough to pronounce their name correctly. What they don't appreciate is working with someone for a full six months who always gets their name wrong, or being asked after a year together, "Wait, how do you pronounce your name again?" Also, it's probably embarrassing for you to ask this question after all that time (at least, it should be). But I cannot tell you how many ColorComm members tell me they get called the wrong name on a regular basis. Either their boss is mispronouncing their name, or they are constantly finding themselves confused with the other woman of color on staff and being addressed by her name. Our Asian members often tell me that the pronunciation or spelling of their names is constantly butchered, or that they have two first names and people will leave the second one off. Yet, for the person on the receiving end of these slights, making the correction every time takes effort. It can be awkward, so women of color just accept it. They think, "Well, that's not at all how you pronounce my name, but I guess we're gonna go with it."

Death by a thousand cuts.

What Is an Ally, Anyway?

So here's what we know: connecting with your colleagues and attempting to understand their perspectives on life and career will help you work together better and improve your business output. Connecting with colleagues means getting to know each other on a human level rather than using this new relationship with someone who looks different from you to satisfy your curiosities about an entire group of people. But true allyship is about more than just getting along with your colleagues of color. It's a bigger undertaking than simply learning how to avoid microaggressions. And it's about more than just declaring that you believe Black Lives Matter, or that you support increasing diversity at your company. Allyship is about action. It's about bringing opportunities to the diverse employees you work with and mentoring them even if you don't "see yourself" in them. If you are on a Zoom call and there are no colleagues of color present, as an ally you will call this out and make an effort to bring one of your diverse colleagues into the fold. If you are supposed to travel for work but suddenly you can't go, as an ally you might recommend a colleague of color to go in your place. If you have the ability to promote an employee, as an ally you will advocate for a person of color. Being an ally means using your privilege and power and capital to advance your colleagues of color, because you know that by invoking your own privilege, people are going to listen.

There has been a huge increase in attention to allyship in the past 5 to 10 years. For a long time, the word was used most frequently to refer to straight allies of the LGBTQ+ community. In 2020, in the wake of George Floyd's murder and the subsequent national reckoning around race, it became more common to hear *allyship* used in the context of race and ethnicity. In fact, in 2021, Dictionary.com named *allyship* its word of the year: "Allyship acts as a powerful prism through which to view the defining events and experiences of 2021—and, crucially, how the public processed them," the Dictionary.com editors wrote. "And while we must acknowledge that efforts at allyship are all too often insufficient and imperfect, the word nonetheless stands out for its role in the path out of the continued crises of 2020 for a better 2022." But the editors also noted that "the top related search for *allyship* in 2021 is definitional in nature: *what is allyship?*" I can't say it's especially surprising. Back in 2021 this was the case, and it still is today; people want to be allies, but they don't always know what being an ally actually means.

Case in point: research shows that there is a significant disconnect between how people of color define allyship and how white people do. According to that same *Women in the Workplace* report, white employees think the most meaningful action they can take as an ally is to speak out against discrimination, while women of color say the most critical action an ally can take is to advocate for new opportunities for women of color. Women of color also prioritize mentorship and sponsorship as key ally behaviors, while white employees considered those actions far less important. This is not to say that speaking out against discrimination doesn't matter. Of course it does. Absolutely. But it's reactive, and it's usually a one-time thing. You see something, you say something. Calling out bad behavior is a lot easier than taking the proactive, long-term steps that will truly benefit women of color and help us advance in our careers. Because what women of color are looking for from our allies is consistency. It's not about doing one thing or creating a single opportunity, it's about continually showing up with new opportunities and taking continued actions on behalf of your colleagues of color. It's about deliberately thinking beyond yourself on a regular basis. At a minimum, allies are paying attention to their environment and taking note of who is in the room and who is not. In every meeting and conference call, every committee or work activity, every work outing, allies are clocking if there are no women of color in the room, and they are speaking up and calling for inclusion. But in the ideal world, they are mentoring and sponsoring and making a point to create opportunities as well.

The Work Is Worth It, but It's Work

Allyship isn't just worthwhile because it will make you a better person (though it will, and that's something, too). Allyship, when executed correctly, makes a difference at the business level. Studies show that women of color who feel like they have allies at work are happier in their jobs. They are less likely to be burned out and more likely to stay at their companies. One study found that women of color with at least one ally in the office were more likely to be satisfied in their job and with their work culture. They were more productive at work, and more likely to have a sense of belonging at their organization. All of this, in turn, translates to better output. Engaged employees are more productive, they are more loyal to their organizations, and they are more profitable. Just as there is a business case for diversity in the workplace, there is a similar case for allyship. These actions, when taken correctly and not just for optics, have very real benefits. But the optics piece is important to keep in mind because while allyship is hard, claiming allyship is easy. It's also trendy. If you believe in equality, if you make an effort not to act racist, you might call yourself an ally. And I'm not making a joke—those are literally some people's requirements for declaring themselves an ally. It's a pretty low bar. In fact, research shows that more than 75 percent of white employees consider themselves allies to women of color.[5] However, that same research found that far fewer white employees were engaging in actual allyship actions, and the actions that took the most work—advocating for new opportunities and acting as a mentor or sponsor—were the least common. Only 21 percent of white employees advocated for new opportunities for women of color, and only 10 percent acted as a mentor or sponsor to a woman of color. (Another study[6] found that while more than 80 percent of white employees believed they were allies to women of color in the office, only 45 percent of Black women and 55 percent of Latinas believed they had strong workplace allies. Something is not adding up.)

Listen, I know that allyship is a lot of work. I don't want to minimize it. There is this notion that everyone should be an ally, and while that would be great, it's not realistic.

I hope everyone will treat their colleagues of color well and with respect. I hope everyone will make an effort to at least get to know the people of color on their teams and to remember that they are human beings with personalities and likes and dislikes and strengths and weaknesses rather than a number toward fulfilling a quota. But I think we are doing ourselves a disservice when we say, "Everyone should be an ally!" because by giving the impression that it's so easy that everyone can do it, we diminish the role and the power allyship has. I'd rather have fewer people declare their intention to be an ally if those who did actually did the work required and did it right. Because not everyone is cut out for allyship, and that's okay. This is not to provide an excuse or to let anyone off the hook. We need big change, and it will take the input of white colleagues to make that change last. And still, we each can only give what we can.

When I point out the ways in which white allyship falls short, I am not trying to shame anyone—if you are a white woman reading this book, you are already starting the work. You are trying to learn about the experiences of your colleagues of color, and you're doing so without putting the burden on them to share with you or teach you. That counts for something. It counts for a lot! But when you're ready to take action, it's important to know which actions will be the most helpful. Like anything, allyship exists on a spectrum. Some people will dedicate more effort to it than others. Regardless of your bandwidth, it's good to know what matters most, because if you're going to put in the time, you might as well spend your energy on the actions that will have the greatest payoff.

So now you know what allyship is, and why it's important. The next question is simple: Are you ready to put your intentions into action?

— 11 —

YOU NEED . . .
TO SUPPORT THE WOMEN
OF COLOR AROUND YOU

A few years ago, a white woman I'd long known professionally made a bunch of introductions for me. She and I had come up together in the communications industry, but she was very connected—she knew a lot of people I didn't—and she took the time in advance of that year's ColorComm conference to put me in touch with some of her contacts. It was a really helpful gesture, and as a result, we got a new corporate sponsor. We also secured that organization's chairman as a speaker at our conference. That was no small thing, because we don't often get high-profile white male speakers at our events.

This was allyship in action: a white woman used her influence to create opportunities for an organization for women of color, and I was incredibly appreciative. If the story ended there, I would be using this anecdote to illustrate all the ways allyship can be done right.

Unfortunately, the story doesn't end there. A few months later, this woman and I were in France for a work conference. Whenever we were in the room together (and sometimes even when we weren't), she used the opportunity to publicize all the ways in which she had helped ColorComm and, by extension, helped me. "Isn't it so great?" she said. "I got them money! I got this person to speak!" Instead of quietly using her privilege for our benefit and moving on, she made a point to call attention to her generosity, apparently in search of kudos and gratitude. To be clear, I had already thanked this person. She did something helpful, and of course I said "Thank you." In fact, I sent flowers. But now I had colleagues in my industry approaching me throughout the week saying things like, "I heard what she did for you—you're so lucky to have her," or "I hear you operate on a shoestring budget." Each comment felt like a little dig at my business, each comment implied that we couldn't succeed on our own or that we only existed thanks to the generosity of this woman. It undermined all the hard work and hustle and heart my staff and I pour into our company day in and day out, and it felt like a real white-savior moment. Back when this woman made these introductions, I didn't get the sense that she was doing it for credit, but now I felt like I was supposed to be publicly appreciating her over and over again. She wanted to be sure that everyone knew she'd done this nice thing for a Black woman, and frankly, it was insulting. Not to mention the fact that yes, I appreciated the help she provided, but it didn't make or break my company. She made an introduction that led to a $40,000 sponsorship. That's a good amount of money, but it wasn't groundbreaking. It was a nice-to-have, but the people who make or break my company are the people who work there.

Allyship is complicated. There are a lot of ways to get it wrong, even if you mean well. I've seen plenty of well-intentioned workers make missteps while trying to support their colleagues of color, only to create an uncomfortable environment instead of a more equitable one. But there are a lot of ways to get it right, too. I promise.

Performative Allyship

Back when this woman and I were in France, I didn't have a name for what happened between us; I just knew how it made me feel: small. But now I know that her behavior falls under the category of what's called *performative allyship*.

Performative allyship is when someone from a non-marginalized or majority group professes support for a marginalized group in a way that calls attention to their own "good deeds." Performative allyship might look like someone wanting kudos without actually doing any real work (posting a black square on Instagram, for example), or it can look like what happened between me and this woman—a person actually does do something helpful, but then she wants to be sure others are aware of her "good deeds." The truth is, sometimes awareness *is* important and helpful. If a white professional sees one ally out there doing the work, they might be more inclined to follow suit. The performative part comes in when you're only doing the work for the acknowledgment, rather than for the genuine intention of making change for another person or group.

Sometimes, people "perform" allyship without even realizing what they're doing. They're proud of having helped someone, so they seek out a pat on the back. What's important to remember is that by seeking affirmation and applause, you are putting the other person down. True allyship happens behind the scenes. It results from someone seeing the value and importance of having diverse voices at the table and then opening the door for those voices or helping them through without calling attention to the fact that they needed help in the first place. Remember, you get more when you give more. You don't have to broadcast your work for it to count, and you don't have to worry that the good deeds won't come back to you. If you partake in true allyship behavior, you have to trust that the universe will have your back. Unspoken transactional karma is a real thing. When you do good work for the purposes of doing good, the return on investment will come. That person will remember your kindness or generosity and return the favor in time. But if you focus your energy less on the action and more on getting credit for your action, well, it gives the whole interaction an icky feeling, and rather than feeling grateful, the recipient feels belittled. The end result is usually the opposite of what you intended.

A few years ago, during the pandemic and in the wake of George Floyd's murder, a white female ColorComm board member reached out to me with a note. Like so many organizations during the pandemic, we were going through challenges—it was hard hosting networking events and conferences when people stopped gathering in public—and she asked how she could help. But she also, before waiting for an answer, wrote us an extra check. She told us she believed in our work and she wanted to continue to support it, so she doubled her partnership for the year. She didn't ask us to publicly acknowledge her increased contribution or call attention to her generosity. She didn't e-mail me every week with questions about how I was using her money or make me prove I was worthy of it. Even when we did thank her, she shrugged it off as unnecessary. Her intention was genuine.

Performative allyship can also come in the form of assuming you know what a person or group needs, and then taking action based on what *looks* good versus what is actually beneficial. If you want to open the door for someone, you need to have a sense of what that person needs. You might be surprised by how often that piece of the puzzle is missing. A would-be ally might say, "I want to help! I want to use my privilege!" and so they'll make an unsolicited introduction, or they'll suggest their colleague of color for the party-planning committee without finding out if that's actually of interest to them. Maybe that person didn't want that particular intro. Maybe that person was already invited into the party-planning committee, but they had a conflict. Before you decide it's your purpose to advance someone else's career, before deciding what's best for them, maybe ask them to coffee. Find out their goals and interests. Allyship isn't a charity project, it's about knowing someone—or a group of people—well enough to know what they need and how you can help them get there.

"What do you need?" is always a more productive question than "How can I help?" It helps you learn about a person or a group, and it doesn't put the burden on them to instruct you on how to be an ally. If you already have a specific idea of how you can help, great. But before you act on it, get verification: "I was thinking about how I could be helpful to you, and I was thinking I could maybe [insert your helpful idea here]. Would that be effective?" This is a great place to start because people don't necessarily know what you have in your arsenal. They don't know who you know or where you have influence. If you offer prompts or enumerate the ways in which you *think* you can be helpful, you are offering a starting point. And remember: when you are thinking about allyship, the more you can tie your actions to a specific economic gain, the more likely it is to be the kind of help someone needs. Women of color don't need new besties, we need upward mobility. If you make a connection for me that will lead to a new client or business, that is creating opportunity. If I get an award because you nominated me, that can affect my salary or my bonus, and thus is economic in nature. At the end of the day, if equity is the goal, we need more upward gains for women of color.

Education and Action

Ultimately, allyship comes down to two things: learning and doing. If whatever allyship action you are taking doesn't fall into one of these categories, it's probably not very helpful. Posting a meme on Instagram is not going to move the needle for women of color, no matter how good your intentions. Observing the problems at your company without proposing solutions isn't going to make change, either. That said, taking stock of the current environment at your workplace is a good first step. I don't mean just looking at the org chart and counting the women of color in the C-Suite. It's going to require more than that. Do your homework and take some notes. What is your company's public stance on diversity, equity, and inclusion? Do they have one? Have they made any sort of internal pledge regarding diversity, and if so, what concrete actions are they taking toward those goals? If they have women of color in the more junior levels but not in leadership, where is the breakdown in the pipeline? What is the history of your company that allows these outdated systems to endure? This might all sound daunting, and that's because it is! It is definitely easier and less work to accept the status quo, but if you thought the status quo was still serving your company, you wouldn't be reading this book.

Another good way to educate yourself is by joining employee resource groups (ERGs) at your company. ERGs are voluntary, employee-led groups intended to foster inclusion. They are usually led by, and made up of, employees who share an (often marginalized) identity based on race or ethnicity, gender, or sexual orientation. ERGs might also be formed around affiliations like people with disabilities, or people who are veterans. If you are not an identifying member of one of these groups but you want to join in solidarity, ask first. Explain that you want to be an ally, and that you are committed to listening and learning on your own. This should be an educational experience, not an opportunity to hear yourself speak. If you are welcomed into the group, attend the meetings and listen to your colleagues' experiences and ideas. A lot of your questions—about what it's like to be an employee of color at your organization, even your questions about the culture itself—will be answered by simply paying attention and taking it all in. I cannot overstate the importance of listening. Then, take direction from the identifying members of the group. Do they want you to be proactive or to take a back seat? If you pay attention, you will understand how you can be of service without anyone having to tell you.

Now, for the *doing* part of the equation. It's not enough to say, "It really sucks that our company is not promoting people of color/doesn't have diverse leadership/only hires interns who look like our executives." To be an ally, you need to assess where change needs to happen and then you need to ask the follow-up questions, namely, "What can I do to make it happen?" Anyone who works for an organization can take ownership of change. In any company or workplace, the people create the culture. If there's a lunch-and-learn or a company outing, it's the people on the payroll who are putting it together. If you want to see change, you have to contribute; you can't just complain. Maybe it starts with informing senior leadership or HR that you want to see a more diverse pipeline and you want to help establish that. Maybe it's vouching for candidates of color who come through the door. Maybe it's challenging the excuse that "we want good people of color; we just don't know how to find them—we never get their résumés." That's a common HR claim—*We want to diversify our employees; we just don't know where to find the talent*—but there is no shortage of talent. At any level of the professional ladder, you can find talent of color. If you take on the tasks of figuring out where your company currently recruits new talent and of identifying organizations you could partner with to bring in more diverse applicants—those are tangible actions that could make a measurable difference.

Establishing goals that can actually be measured is another critical piece of creating a more equitable environment. Too often, you see a company express outrage after something happens in the news—an unarmed Black man is shot; some other racist action is caught on video— and they publicly vow to create change without pledging any specific or measurable actions. Three months later, the news cycle has turned to a different hot topic and suddenly the company no longer has the bandwidth for all those pledges they once made. Real organizational change is not about a PR campaign, it's about setting goals for which you can assess progress over time. Change that cannot be measured will never happen. You want to lose weight? By when? Where did you start? What is your goal? Without accountability, you are having the same conversations year after year and frankly, that's usually what happens when it comes to the diversity conversation. Good intentions, measly results.

If this kind of organizational involvement feels too overwhelming for your first foray into allyship, you can absolutely start smaller. Maybe your first step is to simply invite your colleagues of color to the table, so to speak.

"Hey, we're organizing a summer outing, do you want to come? Do you want to help organize?" But don't only invite one person. Including one token person of color is not a genuine effort, and when you do something only for optics, your colleagues of color will not be fooled. Put forth a real effort to diversify the event. If the people you invite say no, that's on them. But extending an invitation is extending an olive branch, and people of color in the workplace rarely get olive branches. So don't assume that because your colleague of color wasn't at the last outing she didn't care to be involved. It might be the case that no one remembered to tell her until the last minute.

I know an invitation might seem like a minor act, but sometimes the little things seem so little that they get overlooked entirely. Everyone thinks someone else is taking care of it, so nobody takes ownership, and being an ally is about taking ownership of change. Extending an invitation might not seem as impactful as making some grand statement in support of diversity, equity, and inclusion, but that invitation will contribute to the larger goal of people getting to know one another. The invitation is action toward a more inclusive whole, and a company is going to get more out of an employee who feels included. When the people in a company invest in you, you invest in the company.

Sometimes allyship can be about the things you do when your colleagues of color are *not* present. When you are in the majority, you are privy to conversations. You know which people get made fun of, which colleague's name no one can pronounce correctly. If you are a part of a conversation in which your colleagues of color are being othered, it's incumbent upon you to speak up. Be the person to say, "This is not right" or "It's time that you learn her name," or "She actually doesn't look anything like the woman you are confusing her with, except for the fact that they are both Asian." As an ally, you are fighting for inclusivity and opportunity, and that starts with respect—and that respect is just as important behind closed doors as it is when your colleague of color is in the room.

In its simplest terms, allyship is about mentorship or sponsorship across race lines. It's about creating opportunities for colleagues of color that can help them advance in their careers. Think promotions, attendance at conferences, nominations for awards or speaker positions, inclusion on high-profile committees, teaching your young colleagues of color the soft skills and rules of the game that they might not have learned otherwise (or gifting them this book!). Ask what they need, share what you can offer, and see what makes the most sense. Don't assume you know what they need, and don't ask for kudos for your behavior. Contribute to the change and know that the benefits of your efforts will come back to you.

Mistakes Happen

Anyone who is trying to do something difficult is going to mess up from time to time. If you are putting in the work to be a good ally, you aren't always going to get it right. If and when you realize that you've made a mistake—whether you committed a microaggression or you took up space in an ERG or you made an assumption about what your co-worker needed—the best thing you can do is to acknowledge the error, take accountability, and apologize. Don't tell a long story to explain yourself, don't make comparisons to an experience you once had, and don't make excuses. I've seen people say the wrong thing or do something offensive and they'll respond by saying, "Well, my other Black friend wasn't offended." Or, they'll try to minimize their error by likening the offense to something they've been through, something like "I know how you feel; I had the same experience when I was the only woman in the room," or "I understand how you feel because my son is gay." It comes from a place of nervousness—someone makes a mistake and they are so nervous about looking racist that they try to negate their error by throwing other examples into the mix or trying to explain why they did whatever they did wrong. Don't do that. Acknowledge your mistake, own it, apologize, and move on. There's not much more the other person can say once you've admitted your error and apologized. If you protest, or you try to explain why what you did was okay, the debate or conflict can escalate, but there's nothing more to say if you are called out and you simply say: "I should have known better. That was not my intention. I'm sorry."

The Work Is Never Done

When I first started in the working world in the 2010s, conversations about allies were not happening. In fact, they were taboo. This was back when people were saying, "I don't see color" as a way to declare that they treated everyone equally. (Hopefully you already know not to say this. When someone tells me they don't see color, it's as if they are saying they don't see me. For women of color, race is a part of our identity. Not to mention that saying you don't see color just tells me that you're either ignoring or unwilling to consider issues of racism and inequality that are still alive and well.) If someone had asked how to be an ally to their colleagues of color 20 years ago, they likely would have been told to "just treat them like everyone else."

I say this because I want to acknowledge that we've made real progress, and of course I'm happy to see it. But the work is ongoing. Today, we *are* talking about the issues—people are aware of the problem and calling for change—but I still worry about whether the work is being prioritized. Yes, you need to recognize that there's a problem before you can solve it, but the time has come for the next step. Systems will not change until the people in the majority start making the changes—not *calling* for change, but *making* change. But remember, you can start small. Do your research. Read more books like this one, or find the articles where women of color open up about their burden. Listen to your colleagues of color. Invite them to coffee or to the office happy hour. Make sure they are included in any space where other nonmarginalized employees are. Ask them: What do you need?

CONCLUSION:
THOSE FOUR
LITTLE WORDS

What do you need?

This is the question that kick-started the ColorComm network, and it's the question that women of color must continually ask of themselves and of each other if they want to advance professionally. Too often, our needs are overlooked and undervalued, despite what is often a disproportionate workload. We don't ask ourselves what we need because we are too busy making sure our bosses or colleagues are getting what *they* need. But if you want to be successful and get ahead, you can't just cross your fingers and hope for the best. You can't just spin your wheels and put forth your best effort and hope that your manager will notice and reward you. Like any successful venture, your career needs a strategic plan, and that starts by figuring out where you want to go and what you need to get there.

Perhaps when you started this book all you knew was that you needed *help*. A little vague, a little overwhelming, but okay. It's a start. Now that you've arrived at the conclusion, I hope you're clearer on what, *specifically*, you need. Maybe you need a mentor or more flexibility, or to manage a bigger budget. Maybe you need an introduction to a peer in your industry. Maybe you need to start looking for a job, or to start saving so you can pursue your side hustle full-time. Being specific with your needs and understanding *why* you need them (because they'll keep you from feeling burned out or they'll help you prove yourself to the higher-ups, for instance) is critical to their fulfillment. If you tell someone you need help getting ahead, well, that's a pretty big ask. If you tell that same person that you need an e-mail address for a specific HR person at XYZ company, well, they either have it or they don't. The more specific you are, the easier it is to identify a helpful source, and the easier it is to get results.

Of course, not all needs require aid or input from others. Identifying what you need might simply help you prioritize and come up with an action plan so that you are moving *toward* something. Because frankly, if nothing else, that's the key to enjoying your career. If you wake up every day and go to work (whether in an office, at a co-working space, or on your laptop at your kitchen table) and you feel like everything you're doing is toward a great purpose, that's how you get rid of the hamster-wheel feeling once and for all. That's how you get ahead, and how you feel good about yourself along the way. Because nothing feels better than progress. And every time you make progress for yourself, you are making progress for women of color. Our individual successes are part of a much bigger story.

There's a reason we ask, "What do you need?" at nearly every ColorComm event, even when the attendees are repeat guests. It's not a one-time question. Your needs will evolve. They'll evolve as you climb the career ladder, because what you need when you're a junior employee will look very different from what you'll need once you get to the executive level. (Though I should point out, everyone has needs. If you think you'll hit the C-suite and suddenly have it all handled on your own, you're in for a rude awakening one day.) They'll evolve as your personal life changes—maybe you'll have kids, maybe you'll buy a house, maybe you'll have aging parents you need to care for—and though this may not be of interest to your employer (you're not going to get a raise just because you now have a mortgage), it will affect how you assess what you want out of your career, and what next step makes the most sense. If you have kids, you might decide you're willing to take a smaller raise if it means more flexibility. You should assess your needs on a regular basis, and revisit the question throughout your career. When you've lost your way, when it feels like the journey you planned is no longer the journey you're on, "What do you need?" can be your North Star. Even one small step in a deliberate direction can reorient you back on your path.

If you take nothing else from this book, I hope you'll remember this: fulfilling your professional needs will lead to a fulfilling professional life. Your career takes up a lot of space—most of us will work 40 hours a week, or more, for decades. That is a serious undertaking, and it has serious implications for our happiness and satisfaction. But sometimes we get so caught up in the weeds that we forget that we (hopefully) chose our specific career because we had an interest in or talent for the work. So as you turn this last page, I hope you feel empowered to do all that is necessary to remind those around you why you're here. Showcase your value, strengthen your relationships, and keep moving forward. Because the systems are not going to change overnight. Cultural change will happen incrementally, but your career? You have the power to get it on the fast track. And if you don't care enough to harness that power, no one else is going to do it for you.

No matter your career pursuits, let this serve as a reminder that you deserve all the success that comes your way. If you've earned it, then you deserve it—after all, you probably worked twice as hard to get it. So go out there and get what you need. It's the first step toward living the life you want.

ENDNOTES

Chapter I

1. Culture Amp, *Understanding the DEI Landscape*, 2022 Workplace DEI Report, https://www.cultureamp.com/diversity-inclusion-report.

Chapter 2

1. Bureau of Labor Statistics, "Number of Jobs, Labor Market Experience, Marital Status, and Health: Results from a National Longitudinal Survey," August 31, 2021, https://www.bls.gov/news .release/pdf/nlsoy.pdf (news release).

Chapter 3

1. Julia Freeland Fisher, "How to Get a Job Often Comes Down to One Elite Personal Asset, and Many People Still Don't Realize It," *CNBC Work*, February 14, 2020.

2. PayScale, Inc., "PayScale Reveals That Employee Referrals Can Affect Candidate Pay but Your Relationship to the Employee Referring You Matters," January 23, 2018, https://www. globenewswire.com/en/news-release/2018/01/23/1298908/0/en/ PayScale-Reveals-that-Employee-Referrals-Can-Affect-Candidate- Pay-But-Your-Relationship-to-the-Employee-Referring-You-Matters. html (news release).

Chapter 4

1. Patrick M. Kline, Evan K. Rose, and Christopher R. Walters, "Systemic Discrimination Among Large U.S. Employers," National Bureau of Economic Research, Working Paper 29053 (July 2021). https://www.nber.org/papers/w29053.

2. Ibid.

3.   Michelle C. Haynes and Madeline E. Hellman, "It Had to Be You (Not Me)! Women's Attributional Rationalization of the Contribution to Successful Joint Work Outcomes," *Personality and Social Psychology Bulletin* 39, no. 7 (May 7, 2013). https://journals.sagepub.com/doi/abs/10.1177/0146167213486358.

4.   Christine L. Exley and Judd B. Kessler, "The Gender Gap in Self-Promotion," National Bureau of Economic Research, Working Paper 26345 (October 2019). https://www.nber.org/papers/w26345.

5.   Shalene Gupta, "Bad News: The Gender Pay Gap Is Even Worse for Freelancers," *Fast Company* (July 15, 2022) https://www.fastcompany.com/90769690/women-freelance-work-gender-pay-gap.

Chapter 5

1.   KPMG, "Risk, Resilience, Reward: Mastering the Three 'R's': The Key to Women's Success in the Workplace," 2019 KPMG Women's Leadership Study, https://info.kpmg.us/content/dam/info/en/news-perspectives/pdf/2019/KPMG_Womens_Leadership_Study.pdf.

2.   McKinsey & Company. 2019. Women in the Workplace 2019.

3.   Ibid.

4.   Hernandez, et. al, "Bargaining While Black: The Role of Race in Salary Negotiations," *Journal of Applied Psychology* 104, no. 4 (2019): 581–592.

5.   LeanIn.Org, "The State of Black Women in Corporate America," Part 1: Problems, Section 4: Ambition, 2020, https://leanin.org/research/state-of-black-women-in-corporate-america/section-4-ambition.

6.   American Express, "The 2019 State of Women-Owned Businesses Report" (2019). https://ventureneer.com/wp-content/uploads/2019/10/Final-2019-state-of-women-owned-businesses-report.pdf.

Chapter 8

1.   Colleen Ammerman and Boris Groysberg. "Women Can't Go back to the Pre-Pandemic Status Quo," *Harvard Business Review* (March 8, 2022.)

2.   Ellsworth, et al., "Why Women of Color Are Leaving, and How to Rethink Your DE&I Strategy," McKinsey & Company (January, 2022), https://www.mckinsey.com/capabilities /people-and-organizational-performance/our-insights/the -organization-blog/why-women-of-color-are-leaving-and -how-to-rethink-your-dei-strategy.

Chapter 9

1.   Alexandra Kalev, "How You Downsize Is Who You Downsize: Biased Formalization, Accountability, and Managerial Diversity," *American Sociological Review* 79, no. 1 (2014): 109–135, https:// people.socsci.tau.ac.il/mu/alexandrakalev/files/2015/07 /Kalev-2014.pdf.

2.   Caroline Modarressy-Tehrani, "Women of Color Hardest Hit by Pandemic Joblessness," August 1, 2020, https://www.nbcnews.com /news/us-news/women-color-hardest-hit-pandemic-joblessness -n1235585.

Chapter 10

1.   Global Industry Analysts, Inc., *Diversity and Inclusion (D&I): Global Strategic Business Report* (April 2023). https://www .researchandmarkets.com/reports/5519706/diversity-and -inclusion-dandi-global-market.

2.   Sylvia Ann Hewlet, Melinda Marshall, and Laura Sherbin, "How Diversity Can Drive Innovation," *Harvard Business Review*, (December 2013). https://hbr.org/2013/12/how-diversity-can -drive-innovation.

3.   Tsusaka, et al., "Diversity at Work," BCG (July 20, 2017) https:// www.bcg.com/publications/2017/diversity-at-work.

4.   "Women in the Workplace 2021: The Full Report." n.d. Lean In. https://leanin.org/women-in-the-workplace/2021.

5.   Ibid.

6.   LeanIn.Org, "Allyship at Work," n.d., https://leanin.org/allyship -at-work#!.

INDEX

Y

ACKNOWLEDGMENTS

What do you need? Four powerful words that have transformed the way we think about our lives, our careers, our experiences, our dreams, our hopes, our family and our reality. Since launching ColorComm, I've been on a journey to be specific about my needs, to get clear about the timeline to receive these needs, and to be deliberate in exiting situations when needs are not met.

I want to thank each reader who picked up this book in search of change and in search of new outcomes surrounding their career trajectory. I want to thank each reader who has decided to take accountability and responsibility for their own career and those who've finally decided not to leave their careers in the hands of anyone else.

I want to thank each reader who has decided that learning is really the key to growing. And while the bells and whistles are nice to have, the way to make true impact is to have a portfolio of meaningful experiences.

My family:

Thank you for your consistent and unwavering support. To my parents, Valarie and Leon, you continue to push me past my limits and encourage me at every corner to rise above my last set of goals. I am grateful for your love, support, guidance, and direction.

To my partner, Alan, you always want the best for me and I am grateful for your love.

To my daughter, Nora, you are exactly what I need on this journey of life. When the time comes and you're ready to embark on your career, I hope these lessons will stand the test of time and guide you along the way.

My dearest friends:

The Spelman Crew: Tam, Lindsay, Danica, Janina, Katie, Nikki—thank you for being my most loyal group of friends. I am grateful for your support, honesty, and trust.

The Whitfield Crew: Kelli, Rachel, Zoe—I don't know where I would be without this early foundation of friendship. You ladies are my sisters.

The ColorComm community:

Thank you for helping me build this extraordinary community of exceptional leaders. It has truly been an honor to serve and guide you for more than a decade.

To my Book Team:

To my agent, Kathy, this journey started with you. Thank you for finding me and turning me into your client. I appreciate you helping me fulfill a lifelong dream. To my editor, Melody, you understood my vision for this book from the very beginning and helped to make the concept better along the way. Thank you for your commitment and patience. To my collaborator, Rachel Bertsche, thank you for helping conceptualize and frame my ideas while keeping me on task to meet the deadlines. To my publisher, Hay House, you've been a dream to work with.

ABOUT THE AUTHOR

Lauren Wesley Wilson is one of the nation's leading thought leaders on media relations, diversity and inclusion, and crisis communications. At 25, she became the founder and CEO of ColorComm Corporation. Prior to that, Lauren worked as a communications strategist at a prestigious crisis communications firm in Washington, D.C., where she oversaw media strategy and crisis communications for international governments and stakeholder engagement for consumer brands. Lauren has been featured in *The Washington Post*, *Forbes*, and *People*, as well as on MSNBC and CNBC, and more. She has been recognized by *PR Week*'s 50 Most Powerful in PR, *Ad Age*'s Women to Watch, New York Women in Communications, and many others. Lauren previously served on the Glass Lions Jury at Cannes Lions International Festival of Creativity in Cannes, France. She graduated from Spelman College with a bachelor's degree in political science and from Georgetown University with a master's degree in communications. Lauren resides in New York City.

To learn more about Lauren and her work, visit: **laurenwesleywilson.com**.

We hope you enjoyed this Hay House book. If you'd like to receive our online catalog featuring additional information on Hay House books and products, or if you'd like to find out more about the Hay Foundation, please contact:

Hay House, Inc., P.O. Box 5100, Carlsbad, CA 92018-5100
(760) 431-7695 or (800) 654-5126
(760) 431-6948 (fax) or (800) 650-5115 (fax)
www.hayhouse.com® • www.hayfoundation.org

———

Published in Australia by: Hay House Australia Pty. Ltd.,
18/36 Ralph St., Alexandria NSW 2015
Phone: 612-9669-4299 • *Fax:* 612-9669-4144
www.hayhouse.com.au

Published in the United Kingdom by: Hay House UK, Ltd.,
The Sixth Floor, Watson House, 54 Baker Street, London W1U 7BU
Phone: +44 (0)20 3927 7290 • *Fax:* +44 (0)20 3927 7291
www.hayhouse.co.uk

Published in India by: Hay House Publishers India,
Muskaan Complex, Plot No. 3, B-2, Vasant Kunj, New Delhi 110 070
Phone: 91-11-4176-1620 • *Fax:* 91-11-4176-1630
www.hayhouse.co.in

———

Access New Knowledge.
Anytime. Anywhere.

Learn and evolve at your own pace
with the world's leading experts.

www.hayhouseU.com